JOURNEY OF
INSIGHT MEDITATION

JOURNEY OF INSIGHT MEDITATION

A Personal Experience of the Buddha's Way

ERIC LERNER

SCHOCKEN BOOKS · NEW YORK

For my teachers

First published by SCHOCKEN BOOKS 1977

Copyright © 1977 by Schocken Books Inc.

Library of Congress Cataloging in Publication Data

Lerner, Eric.
    Journey of insight meditation.

        1. Lerner, Eric. 2. Buddhists—United States
        —Biography. 3. Meditation (Buddhism) I. Title.

    BQ970.E777A34   294.3'4'3   76-49726

Manufactured in the United States of America

Illustrations courtesy of the Insight Meditation Society

Contents

Acknowledgments

To Chris Fiore, Parker Ladd, Stephen Levine and Léon King whose insights helped create this book.

Introduction

As the world advanced into the early seventies I felt strangely dislocated. I really couldn't accept that the sixties had so quickly become an "era" in the past tense. I tried to remind myself that, if only for a brief time, the mind of my generation had been wide open to experiences, perceptions of the universe and modes of life whose power and truth contradicted a lifetime of convention. For a while, through chemicals, a wholly other state of being seemed possible. In the initial hour's rush of my first dose of mescaline, that surge in which my perceptions set out on their own, I was freed for the first time from my conceptions, and the world of accomplishment and prestige became someone else's bad dream. But somehow, I was still the same. Despite the incredible visions of Truth I had experienced, I was no more peaceful or loving than ever, and as the visions became memories, I began to experience the most profound disorientation.

Nothing made sense. Almost overnight I had given up most

of the beliefs and operating principles of twenty years. I was ready to give up old explanations as long as I had a new one. But mescaline is strangely silent. Nothing hangs together long enough to be coherent. The friend who had guided me on my drug travels was a spiritual teacher who specialized, like Siva, in the destruction of concepts. When I visited him in the hospital where he was recovering from a nervous breakdown, he had little to say.

Reluctantly, I turned to the mind-expanding movement whose style had always repelled me. Like the drugs that spawned it, the culture was effusive, vague, and hard to incorporate into a steady diet. The psychedelic experts were children like myself, groping with strange substances and playing with practices imported from other cultures. It was obvious that few of them or any other Westerners had ever journeyed beyond the horizons of the rational mind unaided by a drug explosion. So in the spring of 1969 I set out for India mostly on a hunch that I would find there a concrete Way, and teachers who could explain to me what was going on.

In the next year and a half I actually got to India twice. I also got to Bali and Nepal, Greece, Brooklyn Heights, Vancouver, Afganistan, and a lot of places in between. It was like a long drunk that goes on for such a while that you forget why it started. Traveling became the ultimate intoxication, and endless psychedelic that made the question I couldn't answer inessential. But as I roamed around the world, I gradually noticed among my fellow pilgrims the same confusion that existed back home, the same tendency to mistake drug-induced mental obliteration for insight into the unknown, sloppiness for freedom, and sensuality for spiritual discipline. By the time I returned, I agreed with the ex-Beatle who sang, "The dream is over."

The seventies had begun, and on my return to America I didn't recognize it as the place I'd left. The spiritual movement seemed to have died aborning. Frustration had replaced bliss, hitchhiking had become dangerous, and long hair was no way to tell a friend. It was as if everyone who had ventured along an uncertain path had become frightened and had turned back to the main road. The pilgrims had drifted into rock festivals and organic restaurants with tenuous connections to the original quest which were easily forgotten. My friends, now either militantly hedonistic or intent on security, were repairing their drug-blown consciousness with careers in law or business. Cocaine dealers and hip businessmen were much more popular than spiritual teachers.

The whole scene made me uneasy. From my confused wanderings around the world something indefinable had emerged to reinforce my initial vision of inner freedom as consisting of more than just diversion or entertainment. But the sense of ease, peace, and contentedness that I had discovered in open-ended living proved as transitory as that I had experienced through pills. I soon found myself back in Cambridge, married, in school again, studying Sanskrit, and trying to find in books, from a safe distance, descriptions of the world that still eluded me. I tried to practice yoga, but it had little relation to the life I was leading. Permanent expatriate status seemed to be the only condition I could bear, so I put all my efforts into making enough money to finance a trip of indefinite duration around the world with my wife. Spirituality would have to be moved to the back burner for a while.

Then one day in the summer of 1972, while sitting in my gallery of imported art on Cape Cod, I was surprised to receive a phone call inviting me to a meditation course in western Massachusetts. The guy on the other end of the phone was someone I had met briefly on my first trip to India and had bumped into a few times since on the streets of Cambridge. He spoke in a quiet matter of fact tone about friends who had just returned from India, where they had practiced a form of Buddhist meditation with a teacher named Goenka. They had discovered that there was an American in California who had been trained in this practice in Burma some years before by Goenka's teacher. They had contacted the man and he had agreed to come to their farmhouse to give ten days of meditation. My friend thought I would be interested.

"It's called *vipassana* meditation," he added, "and they say it's really practical."

The strange name rang a bell. Though I told my friend I would call back after asking my wife whether she could run the gallery in my absence, I knew I would be there.

1

The Dharma of an Aerospace Engineer

ABOUT A DOZEN of us sat cross-legged in a darkened living room in a Massachusetts country home, attentive to the speech of a man whom all present including myself would agree was a highly unlikely candidate for a meditation teacher. His name was Robert Hover, and he was an aerospace engineer from Los Angeles. He had the incongruity of a centaur. The bottom part of him looked right, seated comfortably on a cushion, wrapped in a Burmese style *lungi*, a cloth cylinder tied at the waist. Above that, though, was a 1950's-style short-sleeved sport shirt and a prominent, clean-shaven face and balding head with a fringe of gray hair cut as close as possible. He didn't radiate beatitude, only practicality. He reminded me of my junior high school football coach. Something about his sparkling eyes, though, the slight hint of otherworldliness, reassured me.

As he spoke his small body loomed much larger in the room, the strong lines on his face appearing like the flexings of muscles of his mind. He spoke about experience, not philosophy or faith or religion. He had nothing to say about God or rituals or getting high. He taught a method, he said, *vipassana* or "insight meditation," a way to see into things as we have never seen them before, a way to know phenomena directly.

I quickly realized that for all my drug experience, Eastern wanderings, and Sanskrit studies, I really knew nothing about meditation, and only a little more about Buddha's teachings.

"I come to you with the Truth of Suffering and the Surcease therefrom." Hover was paraphrasing the words spoken by the Buddha 2500 years ago, but the words came not from his lips, but from within him.

"All Is Suffering." This was the Buddha's first pronouncement, the first of the Four Noble Truths that describe reality as he came to know it. This whole world we've looked upon with so much desire is only suffering. To be born, to grow old, to become ill, to die; it is all suffering.

I chafed under the accusation, rummaging about for exceptions to his sweeping damnation. The eerie, harsh way Hover said the word "suffering" dissociated it from all my prior connotations. And when he pronounced the original Buddhist term for it, *dukkha*, it rang like a curse. "Dis-ease, unsatisfactoriness, discontentedness," he intoned. Wait a minute, I thought, that's not true, I've been happy. Specific instances even came to mind. "And," Hover added, as if he'd heard me, "if you didn't, even just for a minute, think that this was the case, then you wouldn't be here looking for a way out." My mind stopped in mid-objection. He had pointed his finger at the restless impulse of my life, that always accompanied me like a shadow, the ever-present need to be somewhere else, to do something else, to feel some other way than the way I felt.

Now it seemed he was holding out some promise of an end to that. I sat up straight, attentive, all ready to begin to change. He talked about desire and craving and the ignorance of our mind that creates our suffering. My cross-legged posture degenerated into a sleepy sprawl. It was late and his words slapped abstractly against my mind. My frustration grew. More words! He wasn't going to show me how to get to that state, that place. He wasn't going to show me what to do. Only more tantalizing descriptions like those that years before had lured me into the confusion of hallucinogens. I felt foolish now, anticipating that I would spend the next ten days spiritually posturing, trying to act as if I didn't crave, didn't want, didn't suffer.

Then he spoke about *nirvana*. Peace. Freedom. More metaphors! The end of craving. More ways I should try to be. I was now desperately tired and hugely disappointed. After a long silence, he said "Let us begin now." Then he paused. It took everyone a moment to figure out what was going on. "Sit in any cross-legged posture that is comfortable. It's of no great importance. We begin by developing concentration, the ability to place the attention on a single point and hold it there. To do this we undertake *anapana* meditation, the mindfulness of respiration. We watch the breath. Don't try to control it, alter it, or regulate it. This isn't Hindu yoga. Only watch the breath. Place the attention on the nostrils, where the breath comes in and out of the body and note the entire in-breath and the entire out-breath and be mindful of the distinction between the two. Don't become hypnotized by it; stay aware of what is happening. Don't follow the breath into the body or out in the air. Stay at that one point where you can feel it striking the nostrils. When the mind wanders off, when you start thinking or daydreaming, just bring the attention back to the nostrils. Now we'll try it for a few minutes."

Try what? Try thinking about this man Hover, think he can teach me anything? No, no, there, the breath. Watch one in, watch one out; feel the little follicles within the nose, he had said. It would have been easier if this woman beside me hadn't been breathing so loud. I wondered whose friend she was, maybe she was from Cambridge. Christ, I was supposed to be watching my breath, and I was thinking about her instead of my breath.

After half an hour I'd thought of many things, particularly

how difficult it was to keep my attention on a single object without it sneaking off into the ozone of fantasy, dreams, and old songs. Then Hover called a halt and we all relaxed as he outlined the daily schedule. It included ten hours of sitting. Meditation began at 4:30 A.M., with breakfast at six and lunch at eleven and only tea and fruit at five until the next day's breakfast. At certain times we would all meet in the large room for group meditation and an hour-long discourse that he would deliver each evening. Otherwise, we would practice alone at our individual places. No reading, no writing, little talking. No phone calls, no letters, and no leaving the grounds, an area Hover said was now "sanctified" for the practice of meditation. There were no questions and we were dismissed.

For three days I waged war with my mind. But when Hover described the process as "putting a ring through the nose of a bull," the metaphors of combat, struggle, and progress made the operation totally familiar. I was operating within the framework of my entire life. Here is what you want, here are the obstacles, here is how to eliminate them; this is what indicates your progress. In-breath, out-breath, in-breath, out-breath. Great pleasure at watching seven in a row. Fury at the thought of my wife. Not at her, at me for thinking of her. A savage blow squashed the image. In-breath, out-breath, in-breath . . . great calm and then its description! How wonderful it was, how I would explain it to Hover. YOU ASS! This time I couldn't even remember whether the last one was an in or an out. How much time did I waste on that thought?

Who was I fighting with?

Somehow, though, this crude struggle worked. Longer and longer spans of attention to the breath alone developed. Finally I became attentive enough to feel the thoughts just as they arose, and then even to anticipate them. I aborted them mercilessly, smiled at my prowess, and was dumbstruck when the brunt of my own assault hit me squarely between the eyes. The sensation was like having my mind run through a garlic press. Every thought I cut off got compacted and squeezed into the point I was watching at the end of my nose. I felt as if I was walking around carrying a time bomb. An imminent sense of terror, disaster gripped me right at the back of my neck with cold damp fingers. I couldn't hear the thoughts because I was fixed on my breath, but I felt them like deathly whispers in the shadows. It created a strange paranoia.

On the third day I told Hover I was ready to leave. It wasn't that I thought his method ineffective, I just wanted to get the hell out of there. I felt that I couldn't last five minutes more as a captive audience to the unraveling of my mind.

"What is it?" he asked, with a little smile that seemed to me a pretty inappropriate response to my predicament. He sat on the floor almost directly across from me. It was difficult not to look straight at his crystal blue eyes. I found my jaw pawing the air for a description. It was totally unfamiliar. Fantasy, sexual desire, the words didn't come close. Screaming want. Steaming hands. Desolate loneliness. Even the feelings themselves weren't the description. The shape of my mind, bent so far from recognition by the pressure of doing this, was unbearable. I didn't know me. I was afraid of me. I wanted to be in a warm bed with my wife where at least pain and conflict were expressible. This state of formless terror was too much.

"You're doing just fine," Hover beamed as if he'd been waiting for this moment. "Things don't really get started in this process until you're ready to leave."

He had just kicked down the wall I'd been beating my head against and reduced me to a rare state of speechlessness. I sat up straighter. I wanted to understand. He wasn't telling me that my anxiety didn't exist, or that I should ignore it. He was telling me to look right at it in a whole new way. My descriptions had released a wave of sympathetic understanding in him that I could feel. He didn't have to say "I know." I could look right at him and almost see his own terror all around him. But not in his eyes. They stayed calm and powerful and determined. He could look right at me, at my darkness and at his own.

He hadn't banished that darkness. Somehow he was making

his way within it. Now I half-understood, but not really because no one had ever mentioned this possibility before. That the fear, the loneliness, the desire *are me*, not some strange invaders to run from. As I was ready to do, as I'd always been ready to do. *Welcome to right here.* That's what Hover was laughing about. It was the punchline to the joke. I suddenly couldn't remember who it was who wanted to leave. Hover didn't bother to ask. His absolute confidence was infectious. I was a little frightened. I was clearly following him now, and he wasn't telling me where I was going. But I trusted him. A complete confidence in another being that I'd never known before. Because he had nothing whatsoever to hide. And he trusted me enough to reveal that fact.

The next day, as we sat facing each other on the floor of his quarters, Hover said to me, "We are about to undertake the second stage, insight or *vipassana*." Concentration, he said, is merely a tool, developed to a certain point, then utilized. Buddhist meditation, unlike other systems, does not have as its goal the development of concentration on a single object that produces absorptive trance states. Instead, one maintains a highly alert, specific type of critical, nonintellectual awareness, which develops *panna*, wisdom. This is the firsthand experience of the nature of reality. There are many objects of meditation for accomplishing this, Hover concluded, but the most efficient, and he emphasized the word, is what is closest at hand, this corporeal body.

"Are you ready?" he asked rhetorically. Fortunately, the implications of making a choice at this juncture were clearly beyond me. I began meditating on my breath. I indicated with a slight nod when my mind had calmed down and I was concentrating on my breath.

"Okay," he said, "now take your attention, let go of the breath, and become aware of the place at the very top of your head." I was so flustered by hearing his voice and trying to remain concentrated that I didn't understand the instructions. He repeated them, and the next thing I was aware of was a tingling feeling at a small point at the top of my head. He asked if I had done it. This was even more confusing. I didn't want to nod because I thought I'd shake loose that fascinating little sensation. So I spoke, even though I was sure that would blow the whole thing.

"Yes," I answered and heard a voice from far away. I was still aware of the tingling. I had no idea what it was. It wasn't like an itching of my skin. It wasn't even really tactile. It was a new mode of awareness, the sensation of my body. Fortunately, I didn't try to reason out the mechanics of the phenomenon.

Hover continued to give instructions, matter-of-factly directing my attention systematically over my entire body, down to the toes and then back to the head to start again. He never told me what to be aware of, just to remain aware of whatever sensations I encountered anywhere: heat or cold, numbness, itching, pain or stiffness, tingling or rippling, or nothing at all. I had no idea what this had to do with *nirvana*, but what I was experiencing so occupied my attention that the question wasn't worth asking. Going deeper and deeper, I peeled back the layers of my body, this solid, familiar apparatus I had always assumed was me.

The next day I sat in my own room intently following the instructions, moving my awareness along my body. Suddenly the surface seemed to break and then I was inside my body as if plunged into an ocean. Fascinated, I began exploring, feeling organs and canals, traveling up my spine and actually touching the spongy matter of my brain, and then sliding deftly out through my ear.

It was after this experience that the pain began. For three sessions a day we all sat together in the big room under instructions to try to maintain a single sitting posture without breaking it for an hour. This was the "maximum determination hour" or the "vow." It intensified the concentration and uncovered the pain. Knee pains, aching back, numbness and burning in my legs, pins and needles in my buttocks, and stiffness in my neck. We were told to go to the spot of pain and explore it, concentrate on it, get inside of it. I couldn't believe what I found. Knots in my body that seemed to have little relation to bones, muscles, or any other physical system. And if I closely examined a particular knot, I could often trace long tails and tendrils of it going through my body. The technique now was to remove these knots by applying intense concentration to them. But what were these knots? They were results of past actions, of lifetimes of actions rooted in ignorance, Hover explained.

Lifetimes?

I stared at him. Everything had seemed so reasonable and practical. Now we were dabbling in reincarnation. It would have been easier to accept the notion from the mouth of a loin-clothed swami than from this aerospace engineer. Whenever Hover said anything, it had a matter-of-factness that ruled out mytho-poetics. He had an unsettling way during his evening talks of shifting gears from reasoned descriptions of the procedure to what seemed like mystical cosmology. He talked a lot about "planes of existence," realms of sub- and super-human beings into which one was "reborn" according to the *karma* produced in this and past lives. It wasn't really transmigration. He never talked of a "soul," or even body that went beyond. Yet clearly he did not consider this lifetime the total arena of this battle. I let the issue go. I had enough problems comprehending my experiences.

On the sixth morning I was struggling with a knot the size of a grapefruit in my neck. The pain at that point was too great to ignore, so I went to it, focused on it, and found it sitting right in my spine. The pain intensified when I narrowed my attention to it, and I felt a little like I was being hanged. Meekly, I retreated, but wherever else in my body that I went, all I could feel was the knot in my neck. So I returned to it and concentrated harder and harder, leaning every bit of attention I could muster on that single, solid, unyielding spot.

I had an amazing perception of "pushing" the pain. I could almost feel it like an enormous boulder I was trying to roll up a hill. My entire body felt as if it was straining against a huge weight, yet I was sitting immobile. An ocean of energy was being expended, but I had no idea from where to where. After all, this knot in my neck was me. What was I trying to do to me? The pain silenced the questions. The effort only increased the intensity of the sensation, until I was sure it could not continue without my head snapping off. This seemed like a real possibility. For a moment I was terrified, then dispirited. Then the pain shot up more degrees than I thought I could stand. Cornered, I fought back in self-defense, flailing ineffectually, then I suddenly let out a war cry in my mind and leaped on it, into it, through it. And it was gone. The knot had vanished. In fact, my entire spine was gone. Dizzy from the exertion I carefully ran my attention down where the chain of bones used to be. All I could feel was a sensation of formless matter, like a plastic bag filled with jello. My entire body was otherwise empty of its former contents. It felt quite pleasant and not a little otherworldly. I thought I'd attained something, so I immediately got up to ask my teacher what it was.

Outside Hover's door three other students were waiting in line to see him, all of them wearing expressions of pained bewilderment. I wanted to whisper, "Isn't this meditation great?" but no one seemed in the mood to talk. I waited for a while and the line didn't move, which was frustrating because I knew that what I had to say to Hover was important. Returning to my room I sat down again, and got up periodically to peek, but after half an hour, only one of the three had gone in to see him. So I determined to sit for a while, and get back to that lovely floating space to make sure that I could remember the details of it to report to Hover.

I got comfortable, closed my eyes, and . . . I couldn't sit still! My mind seemed full of exploding popcorn. And my knees were on fire. After half an hour I'd visited every country I'd ever traveled to, changed the set of my legs half a dozen times, and was ready to scream. What could I tell Hover? My body was full of nothing . . . an hour ago back in my room? I lay down flat on my back and breathed deeply. All I wanted to do was watch the sensations in my body. That's what Hover had told us to do, and it was interesting. Yet something kept getting in the way—my mind. Not just as a distraction. It was more violent than that. The mind's voice could push or pull my attention in any direction, no matter what I tried to do. I'd been riding its roller coaster for days now. Intense, supreme joy and excitement followed by the most numbing depression of my life. And each state had seemed positively like the end of the road.

Despair and elation. Of course, it was no different than my life had ever been. Only sharper, clearer, faster. Stripped of the ability to act out my reactions to the emotions and the mind states, I could only be aware of them. And suffer them. It was pain. Even the joy became painful, because I knew that the crash was imminent. My entire mind was a huge headache.

I felt exhausted and confused. I hadn't slept in nights, beset by the most horrible dreams of my life. In them a good friend felt I'd cheated him out of some money. I was in a dark room at the top of a narrow staircase that suddenly creaked heehaw noises under the weight of many feet. My friend was with two others. I stood in the hallway for a minute and felt their hatred rising up at me. I saw a knife in someone's hand, and the absolute terror of dying took control of my actions. I rummaged frantically through drawers until I found a big, sharp butcher's cleaver and struck out with it, splitting a skull, then pushing another man over the banister, and finally hacking the last, my friend, until he was dead.

What did it mean?

"Nothing, only clinging," Hover said, calmly smiling at me as if I'd just related a dream about a walk in the woods. "You've come face to face with the most basic attachment there is, to your own life, and you've seen the violence it can inspire." I couldn't even look at him. I felt totally miserable. "We're here to end clinging. To end it, though, we have to uncover it. That's what this process is all about, uncovering and facing just who you are."

2

Siva's Smile

IT TOOK A COUPLE of months to
get used to the lack of drama that each hour of the ten-day retreat had contained. Hover had not given me much advice as to
what to do next, except to keep sitting. Often I had no idea
what I was doing, but I kept doing it at least one hour a day and
although P, my wife, didn't participate, she respected my effort.
I hadn't sat this evening, though, due to the rush of getting dinner before P and I went out. Now I wished I had. I wished I
could be somewhere dark and quiet where I could close my
eyes.

"You all set here?"

I looked up startled as if awakened from a dream. Music was
throbbing all around me, the faces of the performers obscured
by tobacco smoke shot through with spotlight.

The waitress was remarkably patient. I looked at my half-
empty beer mug and started to lean across the table, but my
wifes's attention was absorbed by the musicians on stage.

"No thanks," I apologised.

The waitress smiled and shrugged, as if to say don't worry about it. She had a pretty, soft face and long brown hair and I felt uneasy watching her slip away into the sea of floating tables. I glanced across the table again at P and the immediate gut reaction that arose ended my momentary dilemma. It created a new one in that, now awakened, I was completely aware of wanting to be out of this place and back at our apartment in bed with P.

The music ended, and P turned to me with an excited smile. The musicians were friends of hers. She was looking to see if I appreciated them. My smile was forced and I don't think she fell for it. It didn't help that I had come mainly because I didn't want to sit home alone. I had also come because it made her happy. She didn't like wandering into crowded bars alone. Despite the fact that she had recently chosen to be a rock musician, and looked and dressed the part, people scared the hell out of her. I loved her for both aspects.

"Ready to go?" I asked, not doing too well at appearing nonchalant. I asked her if she wanted another drink. She shook her head. My discomfort was too apparent. It surprised me. I used to feel quite at home in the soft fog of alcohol through which the faint outline of illicit undertakings were still visible. Now instead of working my way to the bottom of one mug after another until a sweet cloud of unconcern enveloped me, I found myself surrounded by the sober, nagging memory of *my body disappearing. All my attention drawn to a bright flame in my chest. My mind still.* I wanted to be there.

I was startled by the thought. In the eight months that had passed since I left Hover, this feeling had never expressed itself with such clarity. But there it was.

"P," I whispered almost fiercely. "Let's go."

Then, because it needed an explanation, "I'm really tired."

Outside in the cold, raw Cambridge night, we walked quickly and silently back to our apartment. I felt awful. My uneasiness in the bar had unearthed my complete discomfort with my present situation. I was biding time. We had planned to leave America in the fall when P finished school. Four years ago I had made my first trip out into the world and gotten as far as India. It had more of an effect on me than chemical journeys. Since then I'd traveled more and wider, and guarded carefully against the growth of any roots. I wanted out. Out of apartments and telephone bills, expensive dope and cold city streets. I could be an unpublished writer anywhere, so it might as well be Bali. P hadn't been much happier with her own life for a long time and was into the one-way ticket idea as much as I. Recently though, her music career had begun to take more shape, so we hadn't talked about travel plans for a while.

I put my arm around her shoulder as we walked. I felt a sigh escape her, or maybe it was me. *Forgive me*, I wanted to say, *for being . . . . discontented.* But the words didn't come. Instead I looked longingly at her, feeling only the gut desire to be closer and closer, to be right next to her, to be within her completely, totally, to experience a completeness that I couldn't find or even look for anymore in words or amusement, or anyone else. *Be here for me*, a small exhausted voice screamed within me. It was a voice of pure pain. I'd been screaming at P for years, but only heard the voice during those ten days of silence on the retreat with Hover. I recognized it now as the voice of desire, of clinging. I didn't want to need her, but I was grabbing, and it seemed to double the pain now to be aware of that.

I wandered around the apartment aimlessly, put on a record, then sat in the living room thumbing through a magazine, wishing I knew what to do to stop the helpless drift away from P.

She came in and sat down on the couch across from me.

"I'm not going to be able to leave in the fall," she announced, struggling to make it sound impersonal. "I realize that that I've been looking to traveling because I had nothing else to do. Now I do. I want to make music." She shrugged. "I'm sorry, really. I know how much you've been planning on it. But I wouldn't be happy going, and that wouldn't help either of us."

At that moment I wished I had had a few more beers. My

sobriety was unbearable. The idea of another winter in New England, trying to write books nobody seemed to want to read, deciding whether to stay up late waiting for P to get home from playing bars with a rock band . . . or to sit on beaches alone, to walk through bazaars picking up trinkets to send back to her. That wasn't what I'd been looking forward to at all.

"I thought of a possibility," she finally said. Her voice was full of sympathy. My pain hurt her. "Those friends of yours with whom you did the course with Hover talked about another meditation teacher who studied with the same Burmese teacher as Hover. He's giving retreats all the time in India. . . . You've said that what you'd really like to do is, you know, do it for real. It's a thought."

Halfway around the world seemed a long way to go with all my eggs in one basket. What if I didn't like it? Besides, I'd been more than ready to leave Hover's course after eight days. I really couldn't picture doing that for six months. But at the same time, just talking about it raised the hair slightly on the back of my neck. In a way it was even more exotic and romantic than hanging out under a coconut tree. I decided to go.

Six months later, I was in India. Curiously, after an absence of four years in which I'd spent so much time planning a return, I now found the mystique of India lost on me. The familiarity of hashish smoke in the hallways and the thin sunburnt Westerners nodding through adventure were familiar yet disconcerting. The temptation of mental anarchy that had led me astray the first time I traveled east in search of a spiritual guide to point the Way no longer had any force, except to dispel my lingering mythology about that first journey.

Outside, it was the same as I stood on a street corner recalling the exhilaration of my first visit. Go to India, everyone said. No one really knew why then, except that that was where it was all supposed to be, and so when one arrived, everything glowed with a reverential light, like spiritual artifacts. Which wasn't bad, I suppose. India had forced my mind open. By presenting me with possibilities of life that I'd never even considered, it had battered the idea of how things should be. Endless options. My practice back then was to try them. My mistake was to assume that the experience itself was the wisdom. Letting go of so many set patterns, set thoughts, and associations, nuzzling up to the chaos, makes you high. Free. But that kind of high is dizzying and if you ever try to put your feet on the ground again you fall on your face.

Now four years later, my feet were on the ground. The last time I reveled in everything. Now I picked my way more carefully and didn't feel that I was missing anything special. I stood on the street corner, with my feet carefully placed to avoid the flat cakes of cow dung, watching the surrealistic juxtapositions of the real India: a bullock cart and a double-decker bus halted side by side at a red traffic light; the mania for personal cleanliness that ignores the casualness of public defecation; the ritual bathing in filthy water. India still made no sense to me, but I no longer found any *particular* sense in that nonsense. People shitting in the streets had no quality more or less mystical than using a toilet bowl. Nothing shocked me, but I was weary of India's recognizability.

The only address I had been given in India was the business office of U.S.N. Goenka. Sri Goenka had grown up a caste Hindu among the Indian community residing in Burma. There, in the midst of a highly successful business career, he had made the acquaintance of U Ba Khin, an important Burmese official who was a Buddhist and a teacher of meditation. Over a period of years Goenka became one of the Burmese teacher's leading disciples, and near the end of his life U Ba Khin commissioned him to continue the teaching of *vipassana* meditation in India, the land where the Buddha first taught. Now, although still involved with his family's extensive business operations, Goenka spent most of his time traveling around India teaching meditation.

I was given these and many more details by Sri Goenka's secretary in Bombay, who, over numerous cups of tea, outlined the teacher's schedule for the months ahead and helped me to plan my "program." It was disappointing to learn that Goenka would not be back to this part of India to conduct a retreat for three weeks, but it was interesting to learn that Robert Hover was in India right then with Goenka at a course in Madras. Hover would be traveling from there to U Ba Khin's meditation center in Burma to spend some time with U Ba Khin's Burmese disciples before returning to India to conduct a series of retreats on his own. All of this was a surprise to me, since I'd just about lost track of Hover in the past months. We had exchanged some letters in the year since our last meeting, but then apparently the pressures of family life and of being a meditation teacher had created too great a conflict and he had decided to drop the latter. I wondered what had changed that.

I looked at the schedule Goenka's secretary had neatly drawn up. With a few days allowed for train connections I signed up for a two-month stretch of retreats with Goenka and Hover at different locales. I didn't dwell on the memory of how long just ten days of meditation with Hover had seemed. The more immediate problem, it occurred to me, was what to do alone in Bombay for the next three weeks.

A few miles out in Bombay harbor is an island known as Elephanta, maintained by the government as a tourist attraction because of its ancient Hindu temples cut out of rock. After too many days in my hotel room, I rationalized a tourist venture as the safest way to use up time. But as I went down the wharf to the ferry, I nearly turned back. All the confrontations I had so neatly avoided now overwhelmed me. I was stopped in my tracks and filled with outrage at the sight of starving mothers begging with babies in their arms in the shadows of the luxurious Taj Mahal Hotel, while nearby, liveried servants walked their masters' huge pet dogs, which probably consumed more food each day than a dozen of these street dwellers. As I stood there gaping, the women swarmed the tourists with piteously practiced whines and rote presentations of their plights. Their mothers had probably held them weeping on this very spot. My outrage now encompassed the beggars, and I didn't know whom to root for. I had as much sympathy for the fat tourists under assault as I did for their assailants. Everyone looked ugly.

I sat in a corner of the little open launch that would take me to Elephanta and watched the passengers climb on. The last passenger to board was practically naked, except for a long, dirty cotton cloth wrapped around his loins like swaddling. His skin, a rich coppery brown color, had a well-worn hidelike tone to it, apparently his principal protection from the elements. It fitted his frame closely without a hint of unhealthy thinness. His muscles were supple and energetic. Like a cat he settled into a neat ball in a corner and surveyed his surroundings. His long, thick, tangled hair was piled on top of his head, his face a thing of beauty with the skin stretched over high cheekbones like powerful drums. The forehead was wide and unmarked above eyes that talked for him. I watched them play a dozen roles. The obsequious fool making his way on board over the objections of the worried crew. The holy dignitary disdaining half-hearted attempts to make him pay his fare. The righteous one surveying this worldy scene. The mad mystic rolling his eyes back laughing in his head. And finally a very gentle, lovely being letting his eyes meet mine for a moment in a friendly, generous gesture of greeting that left me bewildered and flattered.

He was a *saddhu,* a wandering, matted-haired religious ascetic. No one knows the origin of these holy men, but in 3000 B.C. Aryan invaders of the subcontinent found them dwelling on the fringe of society in forests and caves. What deity a *saddhu* may worship or what specific yogic practices he may undertake are really secondary to his way of life. His abandonment of all social institutions—home, family, means of livelihood—is his real vehicle for transcendence. He ignores society and he carries no baggage through the doorway to another reality. Yet Indian society even today recognizes in the seemingly antisocial activities of these religious men some value for the society as a whole, and supports their existence by alms.

The boat pulled into the dock at Elephanta. The *saddhu* leaped off gingerly and was gone down the quay, singing and laughing, before I could formulate any strategy to remain in his company. I spent the next hour leaning against a wall in a cool cave staring at an enormous three-dimensional image of Siva's head carved out of a rock. With a cool, detached upward curve to the edge of the mouth, the smiling face seemed bemused by my predicament.

Outside the cave it was warm and breezy. There were shady trees everywhere. I set off around the edge of the hill. A short way down the trail, I heard a voice bellowing out a song. About fifty feet away from me, I saw the *saddhu* near the mouth of another cave, in a nook formed by two perpendicular rock walls. Naked except for a little swatch of cloth that covered his crotch, he was pouring water over his head from a bucket brought by a serving woman. Our eyes met and he smiled. Without thinking, I walked over to him.

I felt a little awkward being a spectator to his bath, but he didn't seem to mind. When he had meticulously dried himself and rewrapped his body in his cloth, he sat down and smoked a few pipefuls of *ganga*, Indian marijuana, all the while staring at the sky, smiling and humming. I waited for the next moment. I knew what it would be. *He is going to ask me for something.* I was a little saddened that it was going to turn out that way, that there was no honesty to be found, and that I would be cast in the role of a sucker. Then I made a remarkable turnabout. I decided to give him whatever he wanted, gladly, and consider it alms. After all, this was how he lived. I immediately relaxed and we began to talk, or rather he kept bellowing his chants. I interrupted him with questions; he laughed at some, and answered others. When I asked him his age, he told me to guess. When I asked where he came from he shrugged. Then he pointed at me and said, "*Saddhu?*" I didn't know what to answer. Then, in an amazing monologue sprinkled with a few English words employed with startling originality, he told me about his life. He had grown up in a rich family and been sent to fine schools to be an engineer. "Study, study, study," he muttered, his brows furrowed, his lips puckered, and his eyes totally crazed in an outrageous pantomime. He ripped his imaginary books to shreds and threw them into the air. "School," he said bringing his face closer to mine. Then he giggled. "Home," and shook his head. "Family," practically roaring with laughter. He looked at his cloth and little bundle and shrugged.

Then suddenly he offered me the *ganga* pipe. I froze. My careful posture was threatened. He wanted me to come closer, to enter his psychic space. What would I do if he came back to Bombay with me? To my room? I thought quickly about my cache of possessions. My little alarm clock. My insect repellent. My multiple vitamins and foam rubber sleeping mat. He might take one of them. I refused the drug. We sat there silently for a while until he started singing again. Then I heard a loud "Tsk, tsk." Standing practically beside us was a well-dressed, over-weight, Western-styled Indian man, wearing a watch so large he could have used a sling around his neck to support it.

"Pay no attention to this fellow's antics," he exhorted me, shaking his head disapprovingly. Then he said something in Hindi to the *saddhu*, which from the tone of it sounded like, "Don't bother the tourists, you'll give the country a bad name." That broke the *saddhu* up completely. He hooted with laughter, pointing at the gentleman and shaking his head in amusement. Mortified, the gentleman silently appealed to me to censure this ruffian's behavior. I couldn't understand what he expected me to do. Then it flashed on me that there I was, dressed much the way the Indian was imitating. I was a respectable white tourist. What could I find remotely sympathetic about a naked madman? At first I was outraged by this well-heeled Indian's assumption that we had anything in common. Then I was saddened by how much we did. All along I had prided myself on how lightly I was traveling on this journey. But lightness, I was learning, is an attitude. Panic over the *saddhu* making off with my alarm clock was about as heavy as you can get. For all my efforts to deny it, I was a tourist. My passport, my thousand dollars, and my return ticket were all tucked neatly away in my pants. But more than that, my itinerary was my protection. I was on a package tour, skipping all those spots I assumed I'd seen before. I knew what I wanted to see, so I refused all diversions. I was taking no chances, really.

I told the Indian man as politely as I could that I was quite all right, and that this fellow wasn't really bothering me. He shook his head and walked off. The *saddhu* offered me a banana from a bunch he had in his stash. I ate it and he gave me another, and then another until we finished them all. Of course, I thought, we're both *saddhus*. Only I'm an American *saddhu*, and being American you don't do anything without being prepared. Especially since I had no idea what I was doing. He had every idea. He had the absolute security of knowing his part in the whole drama, even if it is to play no part. His every move, every gesture, every breath was his practice. For me it was all groping, seeking to establish an identity. His whole life was about giving up things, letting them go. Renunciation, not denial. I looked again at this man with no name. He pointed to his unhappy, confused countryman walking off in the distance, and emitted a sigh that was full of compassion and relief.

I was in India to meditate. To practice or to study meditation. I rolled the phrases around, seeing which might come off my tongue most easily if someone should ask. Actually I was waiting for someone to ask. I sat alone at one of four booths in a tiny closet of a snack bar that was the hottest spot in town, catering to the foreign clientele with a menu of fruit juices and milk shakes artfully tailored to the appetites of a particular state of mind. They still tasted good to me, though my mind was unaltered. I wondered why it was. I wondered why I hadn't talked to anyone in three days. And I truly wondered what I was doing here. In the close, hungry junkie faces, unadorned, despite their bells and beads, or in the well-fed mindless smiles of hashish vacationers, I knew I would find no answer. I got up, paid the Indian man named Dipti and answered his smile with my own, not sure if his was a sign of a compact of sanity, or bemusement at my predicament. Then I was on the street in the dark, aware of the danger of looking for meaning in a smile.

I walked into the Bombay hotel room and tried not to notice it. It had the dimensions of a cell for solitary confinement, with bars on the windows and a trellis of sweating pipes.

Two weeks after my arrival in India I was still in Bombay, waiting for the man I had come to India to see. Frightened by how much I wanted to be in the company of people, I forced myself to stay alone, apart, silent. I knew before I left America that this part of it would be at least as difficult as sitting cross-legged for ten hours a day. Being by myself. Waking up in the morning without a familiar body there beside me, the constant thread that links one day to the next. Feeling the eeriness of experience passing through me without the comforting echo of companionship, without a second opinion, each decision my own, the freedom weighed heavily. And yet, without understanding just why, this seemed so essential to my being here. The suffering and the end of suffering, that's what it is all about, Hover had said. For me the suffering had always manifested itself as a tangle, a blurry confusion in my mind in the presence and closeness of others, and a haunting emptiness in their absence.

Biding time now in a strange, hot city, I found that this emptiness would sometimes come creeping out of the walls and frighten me out of the hotel room. For some reason it was hardest at dusk. I'd be all right during the day, slowly running my carefully organized errands, working my way through three meals, reading as much as I could, and meditating for the rest. And then the air would start to cool, and the gentle breeze off the harbor would whisper to me, until I found myself beside the water under a purple, hazy sky trying to swallow the lump in my throat. I watched the groups of laughing good-timers and I wondered why I was so insistent on being miserable. Then their tinkling bells and good smells would overcome me and I'd soon be part of their conversation and company. But it would take only an instant, a few foolish words, a puff of closeness to recognize the hollowness, to be reminded that what I wanted, had always wanted, was not within this realm at all, and that to even begin to approach it, I would have to turn from the diversions and accept solitude until I could learn simply to be alone.

3

A Peacock is More Than a Bird

IN MID-NOVEMBER, after nearly three weeks of waiting, I finally took a train to a small city in Gujarat state in the far west of India. It was the nicest time of the year in that part of the country. The weather was warm and dry with an empty blue sky all day, and the area had a different feel to it than any place I had been. It was less intense, almost relaxed, and without the air of desperation that much of India had those days, as its economy teetered toward collapse.

It was early in the afternoon when I arrived at the surprisingly clean and uncrowded station. The buses that went to the small town where the retreat was to be held didn't leave until later. So I parked my bags in the station master's office and began wandering around. Before long I bumped into a small group of Westerners who were clearly in the station for the same reason that I was. They were friendly enough toward me as a newcomer, but as I listened to their conversation I found it disturbing, especially when they talked about the teacher we had all come to see. They referred to "Goenka-ji," with a special emphasis on the last syllable, a Hindu honorific, that contained a strange mixture of reverence, possessiveness, and familiarity. Their strong identification with him set up a protective barrier around them. Tacitly, they were asking, are you one of us? I stepped back, instinctively. I had trouble accepting as genuine the unreserved adulation that permeated their words. It seemed an unnecessary affectation. Hover had taught me a method to use on my own and I had felt very comfortable in the independence of that practice. Now suddenly, I was confronted with a coterie. I wandered back to fetch my bags wondering if the initiation fee was more than I wanted to pay.

As I walked into the station master's barn, a smiling, suntanned Westerner sitting at the table looked up at me.

"Oh, you must be Eric Lerner," he said. He looked familiar, yet after a minute of trying to recall him, it was clear that we'd never met. The story, of course, was that he'd seen my name on the list of passengers on the train to Benares ten days hence. He was trying to get a place on that train. His problem was that traveling third class he couldn't make a reservation this far in advance, while if he waited until the end of the course the booking would be full. I suggested that he make a first-class reservation as I had, but he laughed when I told him how much it cost. Without even thinking, I offered him a hundred rupees to pay the difference. Almost as casually as we'd been introduced, he accepted; and as I handed him the bills, I realized I'd never given money away like this before. I wondered where the second thoughts were.

His name was Travis and as we walked around the train station I was conscious of how at ease his presence made me feel. I recognized him. Not just in that moment when I was sure we already knew each other, but in his familiarity to me. Now it was very clear why all these other Westerners seemed like strangers to me, much stranger than Indians. They weren't familiar to themselves. They knew who they didn't want to be, but their past identities as overeducated, well-fed kids clung to them, and gave their spirituality an uneven, ragged edge. They were tense, because they were trying too hard. Travis wasn't trying. Even though he dressed in the homespun cotton pajama clothing of India's lower castes, unlike most Westerners he looked comfortable rather than costumed in them. His body radiated a certain vibrant energy which most Westerners in India lacked, either from drugs, poor health, or a subtle attempt to escape from the particular physical circumstances they were born into this lifetime. Travis was perfectly accepting of his circumstances. Neither the inflections of his voice nor his gestures were loaded with borrowed Indianisms. His suntanned healthy look of a tourist enjoying his stay reminded me how much basketball and body surfing still meant to me.

At the same time, though, he was in the midst of a pretty rigorous spiritual discipline. He had just arrived here following a twenty-five-day retreat with Goenka, and after ten days in this place he planned on at least a month more of this intensive sitting in Benares. And then?

"I don't know," he laughed, blue gray eyes bright with the humor with which he embraced this whole adventure. "It could be the beach in Goa or a Buddist monastery after that."

Goenka was not among the passengers on the late-afternoon express from Bombay, the last train of the day. The assembled group of students and the Indian course organizers waiting on the station platform were momentarily at a loss. The Indians regained their composure quickly, though, and with smiles and assurances bustled us all off into their cars and drove us to the place where the course would be held, a very old Jain temple in a semiarid plain, far from any surrounding towns.

The Jains go back as far as the days of Buddha, twenty-five hundred years ago. Mahavhira, the founder of the sect, taught an austere practice that centers around the concept of *ahimsa*, noninjury or nonviolence. His followers carry it out to the extreme. As well as not eating meat or killing any living thing, Jain monks wear gauze cloths over their mouths like surgical masks so as not to even inhale a flying insect. They religiously strain all their drinking water and carry small brooms to sweep the path before them so as not to step on any living creature. Like all of India's religious groups, the Jains have undergone quite a transformation over the centuries. Today in India they are known not for their austerities, but rather for the large economic, political, and social influence they have in relation to their relatively small numbers. They are a very tight-knit community, and I couldn't understand why some forty distinguished members of the local Jain priesthood, both monks and nuns, were participating in the meditation course conducted by a caste Hindu delivering the teachings of the Buddha.

The temple seemed the perfect site for a retreat. Drab stone exteriors hid marble floors, vibrantly colored wall murals, and latticelike stone carvings within. The large central meeting hall and a small courtyard set aside for the course were surrounded by sleeping cottages, and the entire complex of temples was surrounded by outer walls.

In the early evening, the eight Westerners and the large number of Indian laypeople who would be making this retreat sat in silence waiting for our teacher. I was busy watching my breath when the side doors of the hall flapped open and the entire contingent of Jain monks and nuns made their entrance. They were quite impressive in their immaculately starched white garments. Most of them looked like they had never missed a meal, and they walked with the assurance that comes only from authority. Their priestliness was unmistakable. So was the hierarchy among them. Four or five fierce-looking older men led the show. A number of Indians stood and bowed as they passed by, but most of the priests did not even deign to recognize the gesture. The monks headed directly for the low tables that lined the left wall of the room, ceremonially whisked their spots clean with their little brooms, and sat down with a flourish. It was clear that they were not thrilled to be there.

I closed my eyes and returned to watching my breath. A moment later I was interrupted by loud voices in the front of the room. Dr. Saula, the gentle Indian organizer of the course, and two or three of the head monks were involved in a heated dispute which the good doctor was trying to move outside, away from the audience. The monks objected to the height of the platform that had been prepared for Goenka at the front of the room. It had been one of the first things I had noticed as I entered, remembering that at the retreat in Massachusetts Hover had sat on a pillow right on the floor in front of us. The sight of a pedestal was an annoying formality to me, but for the Jains it seemed to be more serious. Goenka, a layman, was not going to sit higher than they, who were monks. They wanted his platform lowered so that their tables were higher. Their anger filled the hall. It was as if they were pointing to their starched white purity as a clear indication of authority. They were not about to pay any kind of homage to this businessman from Bombay named Goenka.

I watched in near disbelief as the bargaining and gesturing went on and on. The more I listened the more uncomfortable I became. I felt like screaming. For years rituals and uniforms and pedestals and bowing had kept me away from meditation of any kind. The smell of religion was obnoxious to me. I hadn't come to India for a guru. I wouldn't know what to do with one if I found him. I glanced over at the exit. It didn't really lead anywhere. Maybe if the Jains just stopped shouting I could watch my breath. I finally realized that I viewed Goenka no differently than the Jains did. Looking at them was like watching my own mind: haughty, dressed up for a party, and displaying its ego. I suddenly felt protective of the empty seat in front of me and furious with those stuffed-shirt priests. At the same time, though, I wished that Dr. Saula would put the damn platform on the floor and make us all happy. But in his quiet, tenacious way he succeeded in keeping the platform as it was.

Finally Goenka arrived. An air of excitement and tension filled the hall, and I felt a jolt the moment he walked in the door. It was an uncomfortable feeling, totally unfamiliar to me.

He was a neat, short, round man. His face was intelligent and handsome, and he was clean-shaven with thick, silvery hair parted on one side and large powerful brows, that shielded his eyes from unwanted intrusions. There was nothing particularly holy looking about him. His appearance was very much that of the successful businessman he had become before undertaking the teaching of meditation. His movements were precise, and in the flurry of activity and emotion that surrounded him, he remained balanced and patient, as still as the eye of a storm.

He took his seat and waited for everyone to gather their attention. Then he began a very matter-of-fact, unspectacular introduction emphasizing the most universal aspects of his teaching, its lack of contradiction with any other system of belief, and its accessibility to all. As Hover had done, he had us repeat three times the triple refuge in the Buddha, the *Dharma*, and the *Sangha*. That is, the teacher, the teaching, and the community of those on the path. After that, he had us take the five precepts: abstention from killing any living being, from lying, from stealing, from sexual misconduct, and from the taking of intoxicants during the time we were at this course. This was followed by instruction in mindfulness of breathing. Then he got up and left. It all seemed quite rote to me, as if he'd given that little introduction a hundred times, and had grown quite detached from it. The distance between us really discouraged me. The lack of proximity that came from sitting in a hall with almost a hundred other people was added to by the way he was whisked in and out by his entourage of handmaidens and kept locked away in a private room. I was told that he really didn't see people individually, except for an hour after lunch when he allowed brief interviews. Instead, he saw people in small groups during the day and gave discourses at night. This imposed distance seemed to set him on an even higher pedestal.

On the following morning we again assembled in the large hall. The platform was empty. Some time went by and then finally Dr. Saula announced that we were to continue with our practice as instructed. He said no more. There was smug rustling from the Jain elders perched on the left and confusion among the Western students. The morning passed and when we returned to the hall for the afternoon group sitting, still no teacher. Finally near the end of the hour, the doors behind the platform opened and Goenka came hobbling in, his foot encased in a plaster cast. He had broken a bone when he tripped and fell during an exercise walk after breakfast.

I felt a little like pointing out to his more devoted followers that God doesn't wear a cast, but Goenka silently pointed out to us that ordinary men don't react to a broken foot the way he did. His enormous good-natured smile said he was amused by what had happened to him, was doing well despite the pain, and was thankful for all the care and good wishes lavished upon him. His smile, in fact, seemed so powerful that it reflected all the concern and good wishes being sent his way right back to those in front of him. His full attention never wavered from the job he had to do as a teacher. He worked at it without pause. When I left the hall bleary eyed at nine in the evening, he was still sitting there, smiling, working, teaching, giving.

One afternoon an accusing shout broke the silence of the meditation hall. I didn't open my eyes, continuing to observe the sensations within my body as Goenka had instructed us that morning. The shout seemed far, far outside. Then I heard it again along with a barely audible group gasp. I peeked. One of the young Jain monks was standing directly in front of Goenka pointing accusingly at him and haranguing him in Hindi. I only caught a few words, but from the gestures I understood that the monk was having a little trouble with his meditation. Nothing, nothing, he kept saying. He couldn't feel anything in his body, and he shouted it as if Goenka were to blame! Startled I looked around for Dr. Saula and his helpers, whom I assumed would drag the man screaming from the hall and lock him up somewhere. But there was the good doctor sitting immobile at the front of the group, not even turning around at the commotion. The Jain looked slightly dangerous, I thought, his eyes a little wild, his jaw alternately tight and slack. I contemplated an act of heroism. I could tackle him from behind and get him out of here before he knew it. Then I realized I was fantasizing as if I were sitting up there. If I was Goenka I'd punch the guy out before he blew the whole show.

Goenka was smiling, though. The smile unnerved me. Maybe Goenka was a little nervous? Then who's in charge with this madman running loose and everyone keeping their eyes closed? The smile didn't waver, it grew larger. It seemed to encompass the distraught monk, envelop him in some soothing balm. Everyone else in the room was trying to ignore what was going on, because the teacher could take care of it. And he did. He cared for the man. Something was passing between them, wordlessly. Goenka was listening, and then he began to chant. He didn't answer the man's objections, didn't instruct him. He quieted his mind, until the man was silent. Then the monk sat down. I looked up at Goenka. His eyes were closed again. Nothing had happened.

The next morning at five, as I was meditating in the room I shared with Travis and a few others, I heard Travis apparently getting up to leave. I opened my eyes and he motioned to me to follow him. It was dark outside and the sky was still full of stars as we walked to the meditation hall. "He chants for about forty minutes before breakfast, you know," Travis said. I didn't know. I had thought that he spent the entire morning sitting by himself. So I had never bothered to come to the hall at this early hour.

I had sat down in my place in the meditation hall and begun gathering my concentration when I heard the hobbling and rustling as Goenka entered. When he had settled himself on his little platform, he began to sing. I had heard him chant before, at the end of each group sitting, but this was different. Homages to the Buddah, exhortations to meditation, and finally some chants in Hindi that were unfamiliar to me all seemed like one long extended song. I recognized some words from Pali and Sanskrit, but they meant nothing. The sounds were everything. At that moment, Goenka's voice, with its deep resonant sound like huge brass gongs, in which nothing was held back was the most beautiful I had ever heard. It transmitted his entire being and when it struck my ears my whole body began to vibrate. Each chant seemed to build and swell like an ocean storm. Each syllable was a unique wave. He hit notes I'd never heard before, bending and drawing out syllables to give each a singular life of its own. Sometimes his voice soared on a single syllable. I felt my entire body straighten up, my mind clear out, my whole being balance on a single point. For a moment I shared that point with him. It was frightening. His proximity and his intensity were shaking an inner hold I had on myself, pushing hard against my shell of ideas. I'd never allowed anyone this close before. I was experiencing pure feeling. My relation to him had no meaning, no definition, and it felt wonderful. I had dropped, if only for a moment, the enormous burden of patrolling my own borders, some imaginary line I'd fixed, up to which I extend and at which *you* begin.

I understood completely, intuitively that the reverence for this man was above all thankfulness. At this moment I felt totally thankful, and that was unique for me. I had already recognized his wisdom, his capability and his power; now, I was experiencing his openness and his limitless giving. Devotion to him meant not what I could do for him, but how much I could accept of what he was giving me. It took an enormous effort to accept it all because all resistence, judgment, criticism, and second thoughts had to go. That's how powerful his gift was. You couldn't let your mind stand in the way. At that moment, overwhelmed by the very simple love and power coming from his voice, I felt, maybe for the first time in my life, the very pleasant loss of my mind.

The chanting ended. Goenka, supported by a cane, got up and hobbled out of the hall. I now faced the problem of rationalizing the fact that I was in love with him. This was no ordinary guru worship because Goenka was not an ordinary guru. I wasn't really in love with him but rather with his teaching. Anyway he didn't demand any kind of devotional ritual, singing, or prostrations which would in any way interfere with my notions of spiritual propriety.

My rambling discourse to myself was interrupted by a tap on the shoulder from Travis. We left the hall just as the sun was rising, and as we walked together in silence Goenka's love still radiated from Travis, who had obviously had much less trouble absorbing it than I. My mind quieted down, and as I looked around it seemed that I was in some sort of wonderland. Straight ahead of us over the far wall of the temple compound, the sun was creeping over the horizon, and to our left, in a large, open, dusty space, there was a flock of peacocks. The power of their presence reminded me of Goenka. Peacocks are just birds. And yet something about the peacock, not just its beauty, but something it radiated, said it was much more than a bird. In the same way that Goenka was more than just a man.

Goenka's chanting that morning became the first full-fledged religious experience of my life. But his songs weren't doing anything for the unbearable pain in my knee. Day by day the pain had been increasing like a small, carefully tended fire that finally matures to a bed of hot coals. I did everything I could to escape it. I folded my leg in every possible position. I put endless arrangements of pillows and blankets underneath it. But it had reached the point where the pain screamed at me as soon as I closed my eyes. Goenka's meditation instructions were to keep the attention moving constantly through the body and observe whatever sensations were there. But after a while it was impossible for me to focus on anything but that burning knee. I felt cornered by it with no escape. Why in the midst of this should I be suffering so? I decided to ask Goenka's advice on a remedy.

I had heard that to most questions his answer was a big smile, or if you took yourself very seriously, a hearty laugh. Nonetheless one morning I followed him out the door when he had finished his chanting and requested a brief interview. I told him about the pain that was killing me and why my efforts to terminate it had been unsuccessful.

I would have settled for a laughing pat on the back and silent encouragement. Instead, I found myself staring into his calm, penetrating eyes with the strange feeling that my question had been digested to the point where he could feel my burning knee. His entire attention was turned on me. He didn't recognize me. Yet he spoke to me as if he were intimately familiar with my meditation and my problems, carefully measuring each word as he did in his chants.

"Struggling," he said, "is not the way to deal with the pain." You must penetrate it by simply observing it. "Observe it," he repeated, "observe the way it changes, observe its very nature with a penetrating awareness. Don't try to do anything to it. Just watch it. As you watch it, go deeper into it." His voice deepened as if to demonstrate. "Keep watching and observing through the subtler and subtler levels of the sensations. Observe their changing nature. *Anicca, anicca,*" he said, repeating the word several times. It means impermanence. And, as the Buddha discovered, it is the nature of all things.

He paused and waited for any further questions. In that very short interchange I had absorbed an incredible amount of his energy. I stuttered my thanks. Then, as if realizing how much lighter my concern with the pain had become, his entire face lit up in a smile.

As soon as the next meditation hour began, though, I tried to follow his instructions, but my mind didn't want to just observe or watch. It wanted to get rid of the damn pain that by now had caused my entire body to cry out until the tears flowed out through the pores of my brow. I tried to pull back and just see what it was all about. But as yet, I couldn't. Then that night as he had on so many other nights, Goenka delivered a discourse that he had probably given a hundred times, but that I felt aimed right at me as if he'd written it out after hearing my question this morning. I was sitting in a hall with a hundred people and yet I was sure he was speaking just to me.

"From moment to moment," he began, "from moment to moment develop awareness, mindfulness, vigilance. From moment to moment, from moment to moment, develop wisdom, insight, equanimity. Experience all the different sensations throughout the body. Experience them all, hot or cold, pressure or tingling, pleasant or unpleasant, with equanimity, equanimity, equanimity. Do not get elated at the pleasant sensations, nor get depressed at the unpleasant ones. By your own experience understand that the entire physical structure, the entire psychic structure is phenomenon, phenomenon. Substanceless phenomenon, impersonal phenomenon. There is nothing that is static, nothing that remains eternal. No hard core about which we can say this is I, this is me, this is mine. All is flux. All is flow, constantly changing, changing, changing. *Anicca, anicca, anicca.*"

This was his entire teaching. Everything, without exception is impermanent, *anicca*. There is no self, no ego, no me that rises above this sea of flux. And with nothing abiding, what can we possibly grab onto and say, this will make me happy? The truth of *anicca* has no exceptions. Everything endlessly alters. That true nature of all things is the same. To look upon everything as being really the same is to develop equanimity. It was this that Goenka, through his demonstration and instructions, helped others develop. "Look upon all things equally," he said, "and you will end your suffering."

From the time of my arrival, and increasingly as the course went on, Goenka's devotees wanted to talk about love. They called it *metta* and spoke of it as if it were a personal attribute of Goenka. They also spoke of it as an actual meditation practice. "He teaches you to give love," Travis said. I couldn't understand what they were talking about. It smacked suspiciously of the "love vibrations" of a few years back, and seemed out of place in this meditation practice which was, as I saw it anyway, a system of purification, of cleaning your mind out. Where did love fit into that? Meditation was about concentration and effort and pain, and now, I'd learned, it involved equanimity. Where did love fit into that? And besides, how does one "teach love"?

On the evening of the eighth day of the course, at the end of the group sitting, Goenka told us to prepare for *metta* meditation. Then he began a short discourse on the nature of love. First he talked about it in the conventional sense, the kind of love I knew about. I give you this love if you give me that love. This "commercial love," he said, is the accepted basis of the relationships between most people. *Metta*, loving-kindness, has nothing to do with commercial love. It comes from understanding the nature of all things. It doesn't lay hold of anything, it doesn't try to change anything or keep it the way it is. *Metta* is love for that which is. It has no desire, no hope, and so, no disappointment. It is an expression of equanimity and appreciation. Its passion is of a kind totally different from lust. It is love with no strings.

Then Goenka explained the actual procedure for the meditation of loving-kindness. It begins by consciously letting go within oneself of those elements of mind that block the rise of *metta*: anger, hatred, desire. Then one arouses the sense of well-wishing, of real love for the being closest at hand, oneself. This surprised me but Goenka explained that love for all beings must begin with that being. We can't love others until we can love ourselves. And then as the meditation proceeds, the sense of well-wishing is radiated outwards, to those near you, and then to all beings.

At first the instructions seemed rather abstract, but I soon discovered that my mind, which had been focused intently on my knee for so long, could literally project a wave of good feeling, like a soothing balm, through my whole body and then out into the room. As Goenka chanted, the wave seemed to be drawn out of me, until it became a torrent that I could only watch. I felt it rolling out of me, intense joy and a conceptless wish for happiness and peace of mind for my being and everyone else's. Goenka had instructed us to let the feeling flow to all beings and I felt his wave coming at me, then other waves in the room, then I could no longer differentiate among them.

When it ended I sat on my pillow slightly dazed, very, very relaxed and happier than I'd ever been. Everyone in the room including the Jain monks, looked radiant and peaceful. When I looked up, I saw that Goenka was smiling, almost nodding. He seemed to be saying, "Amazing, isn't it?" It was. I had no idea what it had to do with that hardheaded, unmystical practice I'd come to India for, but I no longer cared.

4

Noble Silence

BENARES, THE SPIRITUAL CAPITAL of Hinduism, and the site of our next retreat, had been one of the most exciting places I'd visited in India or anywhere else in my travels around the world four years earlier. It's a city of death and rebirth. Pilgrims gather there to bathe away their sins in the holy Ganges riverwaters and then patiently await the end of this life in order to be cremated beside the Mother of Waters. *Saddhus* and holy men mingle freely with the poor and the well-to-do. Everyone is a beggar at the end. The fires of cremation along the river banks produce eerie, smoky sunsets while the holy chanting of "Hare Krishna," "Hare Krishna" goes on night and day.

Travis and I heard the chanting as soon as we stepped off the train. We'd been on the move across the northern plain of India for over two days. We had traveled first class so it had been reasonably comfortable, but it was sixty hours of riding all the same. Now it was the dead of night and we were both tired.

We looked at each other trying to decide exactly what to do next.

"Well?" I asked.

Travis hesitated. "It wouldn't be bad, you know, to lay up in a hotel for a few days, see the sights, and hang out by the river. Recuperate after the journey. I haven't been here in a few years. We'll be sitting all month. Nothing lost if we arrived at the retreat a few days late." Train whistles and shuffling porters seemed to say, Get moving. "The course started this evening," I said, slightly dazed by the unexpected choice.

"Let's go," Travis replied quickly. "It's much easier just to follow the schedule than make decisions."

So we got into a pedicab and rolled through black, sleeping streets. Funny, I thought, I'll see nothing of this city. Just the inside of a walled enclosure for a month. The contrast with my past adventures of travel was startlingly comfortable. After the retreat with Goenka I had felt compliant, willing to stay still, not wanting to go anywhere. Walls were secure. We took our gear off the pedicab and banged on the tin door. It was four in the morning. People were awake already. A thin, smiling Westerner let us in, then locked the door behind us.

The activity going on within this Buddhist monastery had so little relation to India that we might as well have been in Omaha, Nebraska. The resident abbot, a round, smiling Burmese monk known by his title as Bhante, had turned the place over to a horde of strangely dressed Westerners under the guidance of that highly unlikely visitor to India, Robert Hover, whose relation to this place was characterized more often by equanimity than enthusiasm. He was a long way from Los Angeles and he preferred bacon and eggs to rice and curried vegetables.

I was shocked to find so many Westerners there. There were over a hundred of them, and many of them were long-time followers of Goenka who had spent months and even years in India. Few of them knew Hover except by report, so the atmosphere in these tight quarters was one of unmistakable expectation. I decided that the best thing I could do, given how uncomfortable I felt on arriving, was to find Hover and at least say hello. Travis knew a great many of the people there, and while he set about finding us accommodations, I got one of the young Western managers to lead me upstairs to Hover's private quarters.

It was a formal room with thin woven rugs on the floor and a single chair against the wall. After a few minutes, Hover entered silently with his eyes down, almost on tiptoe, and seated himself in the chair. Only when he had carefully arranged his *lungi* around his feet did he look up. Recognizing me immediately, he jumped out of the chair and grabbed my hand.

"Eric, how are you?" he asked with a kind of casual surprise at our meeting unexpectedly halfway around the world.

His blue eyes seemed to have deepened a hundred times since the last time we had met. We stood there a little awkwardly for a moment until I finally pointed to his chair. Then he sat down and I made myself comfortable on the floor. As I rambled on, reciting the details of my life since our last meeting, he nodded and laughed appreciatively, leaning forward in his chair. Finally he dropped his feet to the ground and bent over so that our faces were practically at the same level. When the chair became a distraction, he slid off and made himself comfortable on the floor. Then he turned to me and began talking about his plans for the course. His manner changed and his voice became different. He talked about "effort" with an emphasis on both syllables that frightened me a little. What he meant by that word was beyond my grasp.

"We're going to get some people out of old ruts," he said with a kind of grim determination. The warmth of his face had now turned to the coldness of metal and the glitter in his eyes was like sparks. Whatever the purpose of my visit I had forgotten it and was now casting about for a way to leave.

"There will be Noble Silence for the duration of the course," Hover continued. "That means no speaking, no writing, even no eye contact among students. It's time to do a little unmasking. There'll be other surprises too."

I was sure he didn't expect me to say anything, but I continued to hold up my end of what I thought was a conversation by nodding and mumbling polite appreciations for his plans until I could find a convenient way to excuse myself.

When I left I found Travis waiting for me at the bottom of the stairs.

"Well," he asked, "how was he?"

"Mad, a little, I think."

"He'll have some company soon. This place is pretty tense and the course just started. Noble Silence for the whole thing."

"You heard about that?" I was disappointed. It was my big piece of news.

Travis nodded. "Some guy told me about it, then realized he was breaking it, so he bit his tongue and ran off. My boy, this is not going to be sunshine and love like our last course. Come on, I found us a place to live."

The entire monastery, or *vihara* as it was properly called, was built on no more than a half-acre plot of ground, surrounded by brick walls that were a surprisingly effective barrier against the intrusions of the adjacent city of Benares. Right across the street was a bus depot and not far away was the train station, from which clouds of wood-burning engine soot descended, blackening the monastery. But these seemed like visitations from another realm. It wasn't until I climbed to the flat roof of one of the *vihara* buildings and stared into someone's living room or looked down upon a tangle of bodies, carts, autos, and animals that I realized how close it all was. A single cobblestone path perhaps a dozen feet wide ran the length of the *vihara* right up to the tin door in the front wall. On one side of it was a covered, tent-like pavilion where everyone ate lunch. Beside that was the central meditation hall, a two-story square building whose lower rooms were used as dormitories. Facing them across the path was an outdoor kitchen and a vertical pile of rooms that housed other students, the teacher, and the head monk. The monk Bhante, seemed to be mainly interested in the beds and pots of flowers that appeared everywhere despite the seemingly impossible growing conditions, and the ten scrawny puppies recently born to the resident bitch. In the back of all of this, between the clotheslines and the outhouses, Travis found an empty tent, high enough in the middle for a person to stand in without ducking, with a peaked roof and square sides halfway up.

"The last space on the premises," Travis said before I could object to the dirt floor. "But I have some improvements in mind. I figure we've got a little time to get settled before we have to become Nobly Silent." While the rest of the camp watched in disbelief and perhaps disapproval, Travis turned up two wooden beds, a pink and white floral design Tibetan rug, a night table, candles, a laundry bag, and a door mat. We had the best accomodations in town.

As we raced around collecting our amenities I tried to keep my eyes to the ground and simply follow Travis. It seemed he knew half the people by name. I knew no one except him. Moreover, this crowd of Westerners immediately aroused a type of energy in me that I had been glad to leave behind in America. I had become quite comfortable with the inner space Indians insist on wrapping around themselves as a last, impenetrable moat against the pressure of the world, and one that allows you to slide untouched, unwatched, and unjudged through even the tightest quarters. Now I found myself thrown back amongst Westerners again, staring at a hundred little expressive dances, each of which contained a thousand different, and often contradictory suggestions of what is possible. I struggled against getting pricked by a smile, a cascade of thick red hair, a pair of flashing green eyes and turquoise ornaments, or a demeanor of wisdom. And then I danced to let them know my name, angry that I had to join in, frustrated that in the silence, without the words for distraction, all the little dances of my mind would finally have to be done.

The deep resonance of the brass gong sounding throughout the *vihara* woke me at four A.M. Travis sat up and lit a candle. It was the extra incentive I needed to begin peeling off the layers of protection that had barely kept me warm through the night. I had never been cold in India before, but now I wondered if I would be one of the thousands who die of exposure in the winter in this part of the country. It seemed cold all the time. The pale, weak sun rode a low arc through each short day, warming the air for only a couple of hours each day around noon. At night it got close to freezing, but four A.M. in the morning was surely the coldest hour of all. I pulled off the socks that protected my hands not only against the cold but against the lumbering mosquitoes who seemed to know that the precept against killing gave them immunity. Then I wrapped Travis's shawl around my head like a turban, grabbed my toothbrush and towel, and tossed back the flap of the tent.

At the washstand the sound of people brushing their teeth and scrubbing their faces seemed exaggerated in the dark silence. These little tasks were one of the few moments of relief from introspection, and people expended ridiculous amounts of care on them. Elaborate hand gestures were employed to signal when one was through or to ask, without talking, to borrow some soap. Sometimes I would just say "Go ahead," in a clear, unconcerned voice just to see whether my comrades reacted with shocked indignation or an understanding smile at a little common sense. But after a few days, this little gesture lost its novelty even for me.

In the meditation hall, my spirits lifted on finding only a couple of huddled bodies wrapped in blankets. I could get up early, even if I didn't want to, because my body clock is set that way. At night, though, it was torture to keep my eyes open, and I often didn't get through Hover's evening discourses and the last group sitting of the day. This morning the hall was lit only by a soft glow that illuminated the large marble Buddha image that loomed behind the low platform where Hover always sat.

Cushions, mats, and pillows, arranged in idiosyncratic mounds on the floor, marked territorial attachments. The oldest students sat bunched around the front, the newest hung toward the rear walls. I had a spot in the middle, and Travis wisely sat a distance away because whenever we caught each other's eyes in the hall, there was always the danger of hysterical laughter.

I sat down and toyed with my blankets and pillow, straightening out a lump here or there and trying to arrange my legs in half a dozen different variations, knowing all along that it had very little to do with the pain I was experiencing. But like the toothbrushing it was a legitimate activity, and unlike pacing up and down or tossing in restless sleep, it provided momentary escape not only from meditation but from the guilt of not meditating as well.

Finally, with nothing else to do I began the maddeningly simple task I'd been at for four days already: watching my breath pass in and out of my nostrils. It seemed like such a simple thing to do. In a silent, darkened room, immobile with eyes closed, all you had to do was observe the ever-present process of your life—your breath. But it wasn't easy. My mind craved an object, yet it was never happy with one I selected. It quickly grew bored, or sleepy, or turned to something far more interesting—thought.

A memory that I didn't know existed was half complete before I stopped and realized that, no, I was not at the small, quiet restaurant eating that meal. A memory like that breaks up easily. But the song I hadn't heard for years, complete with all four stanzas, bass line, and guitar solo, was harder to turn off. It just kept on playing, bringing with it a rush of warm feelings for another place, another time. But this indulgence in memory had its price, for the fantasy overcame me. I wanted to be there, not here. In a few short breaths I recognized the ordinary pattern of my mind, its inability to experience the present fully, its incessant desire for something *else*, something other than what is. That was why I tried to do this practice. Because there is an ability, I was told, to put your attention where you want it to be. Right here, right now. As the hours went by I began to experience just a little of this state of concentration and its results.

At first it was simply no fun at all. I felt as if I was the Zen master's only pupil, being whacked constantly with a stick to remind me of the object of attention. My body grew stiff and achy. But then the process started to deepen. It seemed that my attention started out just skimming the surface, lightly touching the breath and the nostrils. As my duration of attention on the object increased, however, I felt as though I was penetrating it. The breath was no longer way over there at the tip of my nose, it was suddenly right here, all around me. And close up it was infinitely more interesting. It held my attention. Each breath became a rapid series of events, and as the attention skipped from one to the next to the next without any intercession of thought or even comment on the process itself, the fullness of my mind grew. There was no pain in my body. An easy comfort pervaded like lying in a warm tub. There was no boredom. My mind felt peacefully alert. The breath slowed, became quieter, and yet my detection of it was much fuller. The process accelerated. A distance was closing. The one watching moved closer to the object watched. Something was being left behind. I felt lighter, almost buoyant, as my chest puffed out and my spine straightened up. There was a momentary silence. The breath was breathing, very, very quietly. And then there was a slight pause during which the plug was pulled on the tickertape machine of the mind. A huge, dark chasm seemed to open, but a moment later it snapped shut with the familiar chatter of my thoughts. Only in this, the *next* moment, did I realize where I had been in that previous moment. Because then, in *that* moment, there was just *this* moment. I was not trying to place it, to consider it, as I was doing right then as I sat. And suddenly I recognized the very nature of this *considering* process that was so built into me that I'd never examined it until for a flicker of an instant it had stopped. I felt an enormous urge to stop it forever well up in me, an urge to return to that instant of nonconsideration, to just breathing and not knowing who was breathing. Suddenly the realm of other-than-thought was more than just a conjecture, another thought. Yet even as I sat with my excitement over this discovery, *no thought* slipped farther from me as pain returned to my body. As I tried to regain that fine one-pointedness on my breath, the noise of someone shuffling into the hall became an intrusion.

And then with astonishing speed I grabbed the intruder by the neck, flung him against the wall so that his head cracked and he would make no more disturbing noises, and then sat down again to enjoy my peace and quiet.

I gasped at the sudden violence of that fantasy. I brought my knees up to my chest, rested my head against them, and glanced up quickly to see if anyone else in the hall was in this position or if they were all meditating. What did it matter? I began again but a surge of ominous thoughts welled up. I wrestled with it and dodged it, and a few breaths later, without even understanding how, I was back on the point of balance. I breathed a sigh of relief, then watched helplessly as my attention turned from the breath to the sigh, leaped back to the breath as if it were a boat pulling away from the dock, missed by inches, and was stunned by the sensation of plunging into icy, dark waters. Images of sexual desire flew past, but the sensation that pervaded my entire body at that moment had only a little to do with physical need. The channel of sexual intercourse seemed as capable of relieving the enormous surge of energy within me as a man with a drinking straw is capable of sucking up oceans.

The tension had been mounting in me for days. At first I had ascribed it simply to extended celibacy. Now the sexuality seemed almost inconsequential, like describing fever by the temperature of the skin. The mental images of faceless bodies joined together was only a product, not the cause. Every single cell in my body was stretching, reaching, grasping. Somewhere deep inside me I heard it. "I want . . . . I want . . . ," but the word could not be uttered, because a word, or any number of words, was not enough. No thing, no body, no person could be enough. The wanting was not a need. It was a force. It felt beginningless and bottomless. It impelled me forward but I had nowhere to go. Nothing to see, to speak to, to touch, and finally nothing to think. As the circle tightened the pressure built. The only outlet was for the force to go back upon itself, digging up and exposing deeper and deeper levels of itself. My head wanted to flop forward. My arms wanted to fly open. A silent cry, a howling at the moon, welled within me.

Words don't extend to that strange territory. Not now or then when I struggled to explain it to myself. The real energy that I felt was unrecognizable. The images of sexuality were actually a relief from the formless anxiety that grew by the hour. Without the familiar names for my desires, I experienced the fear of the nameless, the enemy in the shadows. I could no longer say "this will make me happy."

As I walked outside between sittings, all I heard was the hollow clicking of my sandals on the cobblestones. Even the nearest objects to me, my own clothes, my beard, felt a thousand miles away. My breath felt cold within my chest. Each swallow or blink was a ponderously inelegant event. I coughed, spat, and urinated a lot and was conscious of my body as a bag full of foul liquid. Everything I saw, felt, smelled, or heard was filtered through this cloud of gray chill, this fog of uneasiness. I had retreated to a tiny forest that was constantly shrinking.

The sound of the bell at the end of the hour didn't end all the pain. It only shifted it to an even more difficult arena. With eyes open I could catch the expressions of my companions and thereby gauge whether anyone else in the room was struggling as much as I. The exhaustion that was rapidly obliterating Travis's suntanned good-naturedness was of no consolation to me. We were too much alike and clearly different from the silent professionals who sat immobile at the feet of the teacher hour after hour and registered no expressions of discomfort in between. They could do it; I couldn't. In these past days that realization had been growing in me and only doubling my agitation. I couldn't do this really. I thought I understood what was required to do it and I didn't have it. Eighty-five percent maybe. The discipline, the drive, but there was a component lacking. Recklessness. The willingness to drive through the pain in order to come out on the other side. But I kept trying to wade through it, to keep my pants dry by rolling them to my knees. I kept dodging with excuses and believing them. I thought too highly of myself to allow myself to suffer greatly. On a high school football field when discomfort reached an intolerable level, I refused to pass that point. I excused myself from the remainder of the game with imagined cramps or a twisted ankle. I carried a burden I considered too precious to damage. Myself.

As we filed out of the hall to breakfast, I looked at the meditators around me who were, apparently, able to do it. I was not like them. I stroked my proud beard, toyed with the agate ring on my finger, buttoned up my tight-fitting leather jacket. A worldly dirt clung to me. They looked like they had been dry cleaned. I imagined them as failures in the world at large, social misfits with bottle-thick eyeglasses and ill-fitting trousers who never went out on more than a blind date in college. Of course they were doing this. They had no choice. But what was I doing here? I had no such problems. Nothing to run from. Why was I staying? Why did I even tolerate this agitation that got so intense that I felt like biting my finger until it bled so that someone, anyone, even one of those smug little accomplished meditators whom I despised right then would notice my blood, bandage my wound, offer me some comfort, and excuse me from the next hour's sitting.

On the fifth night, at the end of his discourse, Hover announced that the next day, for one day only, Noble Silence would be lifted during nonmeditation hours, though those who wished to could continue to observe it. For the first time I recognized that I was not alone in feeling the increasing level of anxiety that was making sitting impossible. Hover was bleeding the pressure valve slightly. Having made his announcement, he smiled, and I realized that aside from the frequent jokes he tossed out during his lectures, this was the first break in the stern demeanor he had presented to the group as a whole. "Drill sergeant" was what those more used to Goenka's relaxed atmosphere called him.

At lunch the next day, therefore, I gave an appropriately intense stare to the woman with the long red hair with whom I had exchanged disturbing glances for the past four days. She sat down beside me. Her name was Angani, or that was the name she was known as since it had been bestowed on her by the late Maharaji, Neemkaroli Baba guru of Ram Dass and others. She'd been in India on her own for quite some time, knew about virtually every spiritual scene, and had plans to return to Canada some time in the future to teach a form of yoga.

As she explained all of this and I asked her more questions, I felt our words bouncing around my skull like plastic pellets. After days of staring at the realities of desire underlying even the seemingly automatic impulses to converse, this obviously calculated man-woman interchange was too much to bear. I realized that Hover had suspended silence not as a relief but as a lesson.

5

Right Effort

Toward the end of the first week of the course, Hover introduced a new schedule for *vipassana* meditation which he had been shown on his recent trip to Burma. It consisted of six hour-long sittings each day in which the resolve was made not to move at all: two in the morning, three in the afternoon, and one at night after his discourse, plus some hours in the early morning and after tea. It didn't take long for this regimen to produce some very deep pain. Shortly after we began it, a rock-hard knot about the size of a grapefruit surfaced in my neck. It grew in intensity during each hour-long sitting until I could no longer hold my attention on any other part of my body. When I focused right on the pain, my body would be gripped by enormous tension and the knot would suddenly disappear. This thrilled me the first time, but it soon became clear that it only meant that the knot would be back the next hour, stiffer, larger, and more difficult to deal with.

One morning I woke up shivering. My head was hot and my body ached. When I went into the meditation hall I could barely sit up straight. At breakfast time, a course manager noticed me swaying as I stood in line for my bowl of oatmeal and asked me what was wrong. I hadn't the slightest idea, but I certainly couldn't eat any oatmeal. I told him that I thought I had some kind of fever. Finding my forehead pretty warm when he touched it, he had me escorted back to the tent, where I returned fully dressed to my sleeping bag. Shortly afterward, a young Swiss doctor who was doing the course took a look at me and concluded that I had a viral fever, probably carried by the mosquitoes. He said that I might be in for five or six days of illness. By midday, the chill seemed to have deepened even though I was still in the sleeping bag. Blankets were brought to cover me and my head was wrapped up, but I still felt intense coldness. At intervals I began to break out in sweat until finally every layer of cover was tinged with dampness.

Early the next morning Hover came to see me. He sat on Travis's bed and smiled sympathetically as I babbled on about viruses and mosquitoes and fevers. "Don't worry about sitting in the hall. Just lie on your back and keep sweeping through the body from head to foot, over and over again. You're doing just fine." Then he got up and patted me on the shoulder. "I'll be looking in again, but if there's any need, you can just send for me."

There were no more visitors. The course manager stopped by to see if I needed anything and the Swiss doctor came with a thermometer. It seemed to me a little absurd for him to take my temperature since the whole aim of the meditation was to rely on what you experience rather than what you're told, but I sat there patiently with the glass rod in my mouth. When everyone had left I sneaked a look at the thermometer. It registered almost exactly 98.6°. I popped it back in my mouth so fast I nearly swallowed it. Ten minutes later my temperature was still the same.

I lay on my back and began sweeping. Before long I located

an enormous knot of pain in my lower back. I thought it had to do with the pressure of my coccyx on the hard wooden bed, but a cushion on that spot did nothing. As the hours wore on, the pain at the base of my spine became excruciating, once again stretched that word to new limits. When I had talked of "knots" before, it had always seemed metaphorical. This one literally felt like a heavy thick cord, a gymnasium rope for climbing, knotted around that spot in my back. The more I concentrated on it the harder the two ends of the rope pulled. Sweat dripped down my temples, forming little puddles in my ears. My back would lift off the bed and an involuntary, low, groaning sound was squeezed out of my chest.

As I waited for the sighs to become breaths again, the dirty canvas of the tent came into focus above my eyes. I knew that all I had to do to end this pain was to stop looking at it. In fact I knew, despite the good doctor's diagnosis, that my fever would be over if I simply got up, took a hot shower, and stopped this whole process. And never meditated again in my life.

I forced my eyes shut until tears escaped from the corners. What was I doing? How had I gotten involved in this endless physical torture and mental agitation that had nothing to do with peace of mind? I thought of Goenka's smiling admonitions to be happy, and Hover's contrasting exhortations to basically bust your ass. I felt incapable of both. I had gone as far as I could go. And all I had attained was dirty, damp streaks across my cheeks that marked the end of my path.

When Travis returned at tea time I think my appearance frightened him. My eyes were glassy and wide, my hair wet and matted, my complexion chalky. I had spent the afternoon fighting a battle on two fronts, trying on one to deal with this endlessly reexploding land mine in the bottom of my back while fighting a shadow war with doubt: doubt about my efforts, my sincerity, this meditation practice, the reality of this pain, and finally my own sanity. I was losing ground. The pain had grown. It took very little searching to locate it, and when I did

I couldn't penetrate it. All I could do was ride with it for as long as I could while it twisted my body and wrenched my psyche. When I could stand no more and had to let go, I knew I had failed.

"Get Hover, please," I asked Travis. He was only too willing.

"How's it going?" Hover asked with a smile as he seated himself. "What did the thermometer say?"

"Perfectly normal."

"How about that?" He reached over and felt my burning forehead with his hand. "Not exactly what you'd expect, is it?"

"I don't know what to expect," I muttered. Then I explained the situation to him. He nodded patiently. "I can't do this anymore," I finally said, hoping I wasn't shouting. "I don't know what any of this has to do with insight or equanimity."

He spoke gently. "We're here to end suffering, aren't we? That's what the Buddha taught, not simply the Truth of Suffering but its end as well. You're suffering. You've discovered some pain within you. Some root of suffering. You didn't manufacture it. You simply developed a degree of concentration that allowed you to see into yourself and this is what you've found. Now what are you going to do with it? Ignore it? Sit there with a saintly smile and say it doesn't exist? Of course it does! Your body is burning from it. So you make the decision to end this pain. Effort is required. Yes, effort. But just because you are making an effort to eliminate what you wish to be eliminated doesn't mean anger or hatred or lack of equanimity. We're talking about a different kind of effort. One that you're beginning to learn about or you wouldn't have gotten this far. So you begin. You face what must be faced, with balance, not with fear or dread or expectation. With simple attention only, you attack the pain and you don't turn away from it until it is gone. Right effort, the Buddha taught. That's the only kind that works." He waited a moment, then closed his eyes. "Shall we try it?"

When I had closed my eyes, reluctantly abandoning a desire

to fall asleep, he directed my attention right to the base of my spine. First he had me explore the knot itself, moving all around it, becoming aware of its density, its specific points of hardness and greatest intensity. "Go deeper into it," he urged me. "Note how it alters . . . how it *changes*."

My legs became so taut that I thought my knees would snap. But I had reached a deeper level of the knot and I felt it pulsing, growing, and sinking as I watched. "Now," Hover said, "try to move it. Bring your attention down, underneath, and move it up your spine. Go ahead."

It was like trying to carry an enormous canvas bag of water up a rickety wooden ladder. I wavered, then fell, then climbed higher, then fell again. And each fall shattered all my bones, crushed my mind, left me so deep inside the pain that I thought I'd never come out.

"Again," Hover's voice stopped the slide. "This time as you concentrate, think of *anicca*, impermanence, even repeat the word." I took hold of the knot, brought my attention behind it, and began to push. Slowly, a vertebra at a time, the knot rose up my spine. My mind stopped writhing even as the pain continued. The sensation was like a boulder being forced through my body. Yet it no longer hurt. My complete attention was on it. Every moment of my mind was filled with it. There was no time, no space for "hurt" to register. There was no separation between me and the pain. Suddenly I understood what effort was, what Right Effort was. Complete effort. Total effort.

"Keep going," Hover commanded in a whisper. "Keep going. *Anicca, anicca, anicca*." The effect of the word was to drive my attention through the knot like a steel spike. The meter of my mind that registers pain blew its circuits and in the shattering of glass and the sizzling of shorted wires I repeated the word, "*anicca, anicca, anicca*," as a simple reminder of what I was really observing. Impermanence. Changing phenomenon.

"That's enough for now," Hover said. "You're doing just fine. Just fine. Keep working, moving that mass down now. If you need me, just call." Then he took my blanket, tucked it up around my chin, patted me on the shoulder, and left me with a smile of perfect kindness that made me wonder why I'd ever doubted.

At four A.M. the next morning the alarm clock went off. I got out of my sleeping bag and picked up my toothbrush and towel, fully expecting to take my place in the meditation hall this morning. Thus, it came as a bit of a shock as I squatted over the Indian-style ground-level toilet to observe coal black feces dropping out of me while my knees grew so rubbery I thought I'd fall in after them.

I couldn't believe it. As I numbly returned to my cocoon, I could not even recall the sensation of calm and certitude of less than twelve hours ago. Twelve hours? Had I ever felt that this was anything but insanity? Had I ever felt anything but miserably sick, fed up and full of doubt? You're doing fine he had said. But now? I searched carefully through my body, found almost immediately the cloud of pain behind my forehead, felt my body wince, felt my mind wince harder, almost in disbelief. Yes, I had fully expected it all to be gone this morning. To go through it all again, and perhaps again and again was a concept I simply could not embrace.

Doubt spread over the surface of my mind like a rash. Little whispers that I slapped into silence popped up elsewhere as screams. It doesn't work, it doesn't work. The protest became hysterical laughter. But the doubt had nothing at all to do with this method, this teacher. I doubted me.

I was distracted from that silent confrontation by the banging of my head against the wooden bed. I propped myself up on my elbow groping for the tent flap. No one was around. It was midmorning and everyone was in the hall. When I swung my legs down, they tangled in the blankets and the bag. For the first time in my life I felt the chilled, clammy hands of desperation on the back of my neck. I was trapped, burning and tangled in my sweat-soaked blankets with no refuge from the fever that was consuming me.

At that moment I experienced no blinding flash of insight, no transcendent wisdom, only the frustration of "knowing myself" at the level that illuminated the entanglement of the situation but not the way out of it. I had shielded myself from this moment all my life. I had always managed to save myself from failure before it came, by abandoning my commitment to a person or a goal before rejection came. I had always had perfect confidence in all my capabilities except one: the ability to survive failure. It was utter fear of being knocked on my ass.

That's just where I had landed. And it didn't feel good. My body and mind had failed. I was beaten and exhausted. All I could do was seethe in helpless rage. I hated this place, these people, and myself.

The fight was over, but now what? The pain was still right there, but the fear of the pain was gone. I relaxed on my bed, calmly miserable, alone with the strange consolation of one who has survived a disaster. In my own personal holocaust I had just lost what I'd held most dear, success. And without choosing to, I'd survived. A strange, empty, uncaring attitude filled me. Let them know I'm not in the hall, not sick and not meditating. Let them know I've failed.

I closed my eyes and lay still. My body ceased to console itself. My mind had little more to say. I felt as if I'd been tumbling interminably down a deep shaft, and now as I lay on my back, all I could do was stare quietly at the pinhole of light far, far above me.

It is hard to describe what happened next. The pain began again. The next thing I was aware of was my attention moving in a steady motion down through my body from head to foot. A certain cheerful exuberance pervaded my effort and it didn't fade even when the sensation deep within my skull reemerged. During the four uninterrupted hours that I continued to work, contortions and chills lost their drama, and my pain lost its fascination. I was operating in a soundless space where my actions had no vibrations, no significance. When the knot of pain had worked its way down to the very base of my spine and begun to grow there with increasingly rapid pulsations so that my body seemed to be drawn and quartered, I simply watched. Then, the very next instant, as I did absolutely nothing, the entire mass came roaring back up my spine like a locomotive with its whistle screaming, leaped into my head, and came exploding out the top. In its wake a wave rolled up from my toes and I felt as if I were being emptied of all the contents of my body through the top of my head.

A few minutes later Travis came in to find me out of my sleeping bag, sitting up in only my light cotton pants and shirt. "I know" I said before he could speak. "You just had a great meditation. Where's the peanut butter?" He had saved some. I finished it and the other food he had brought. Then I collapsed into sleep.

I woke up twelve hours later, took a shower and shaved, and dressed in clean white clothes. Then, barefoot despite the cold, I went to see Hover.

"What was it?" I asked him even before I said hello. He was staring at my face and looked pleased. I felt a little self-conscious, but also aware that I probably did "look" different. It had to show. I felt about fifty pounds lighter, and as though my feet were not quite touching the ground. A warmth seemed to be radiating out from my skin for a good couple of inches.

"What difference does it make?" Hover finally shrugged. "What will labeling it do? What we're interested in here is the process, the development of a state of mind in response to phenomena—mental and physical. Don't confuse the effects you see with the process of insight itself."

That night I learned a little more about effects when Hover told the group the story of his own life and his experiences with his teacher, U Ba Khin. "I was the first Western engineer to ever hit the International Meditation Center in Rangoon," Hover related. The impression he gave was that none of it was meant to be, yet it had all come to pass. He was a research specialist for North American Aviation Corporation, a martini-drinking, cigar-smoking father of four, whose only knowledge

· 60 ·

of Buddhism, as he put it, "was how to spell it." Simply from speaking a few words with an acquaintance who had just returned from a visit to the Center in Rangoon, he carefully arranged to step out of his life for a month to fly halfway around the world for meditation, when that word hadn't even popped up yet on the borders of American consciousness. Once he arrived in Rangoon, almost from the moment he sat down, it was perfectly clear that he would have to face extraordinary obstacles to his practice. All he had going for him, it seemed, was effort.

"I was a five-pillow man," Hover described. "One under my seat, one under each knee, one behind my back against the wall, and one that I brought along," and he waved his hand in the air shaking an imaginary pillow that you could practically see, "just in case." He demonstrated his initial sitting posture: slumped shoulders, knees jutting up in the air, and an expression of naive bewilderment on his face.

He recalled the actual physical manifestations he went through: the pain-locked joints, the contortions he thought would break him in two as they bent his body into positions that could not be duplicated, the sensation of having his skin lump up as if pencil erasers were being pushed outward from within his body, two changes of clothing a day as he soaked through them with sweat within a few hours. "In fact," he finally said, "there is nothing that any of you have told me about that I didn't go through. Physical and otherwise." He paused and took a breath. "There are crows that live in the trees surrounding the Center in Rangoon, big black birds," he began once again. "And you can hear them at almost any time of day. Once as I lay in my sleeping quarters I looked up and saw one flying by. Saw it clearer than I've ever seen anything. As I stared at it, I was staring clean through it, as if looking at an X-ray picture, and I could see its flight slowed down, each movement separated into a hundred distinct moments."

Suddenly he raised his arms like the big wings of those crows, his head was altered and his body seemed to be buoyed off his pillow. Then he flapped his arms slowly, tick-te-tick-te-tick-te-tick, like a series of pictures flashed in rapid succession on a screen. "And then I heard its cry. And it was like I'd never heard a crow's voice before, 'Caw·ca-ca-ca-caw, ca-ca-*caw*-ca ca-ca, ca-ca-ca-CAW' and it was no ordinary sound. It was a cry for help, to escape. It was the cry of suffering. Of *dukkha*."

6

Why the Buddha Sat Under a Tree

Iᴍᴍᴇᴅɪᴀᴛᴇʟʏ ᴀғᴛᴇʀ Hᴏᴠᴇʀ'ꜱ departure I had begun another retreat, and on New Year's Day Goenka's chanting brought to an end forty continuous days of meditation behind walls for me. An hour after the meditation ended, my monastic woolen shawl and white cotton pajama suit were tucked away in my bag, and I marveled at the strange feel of denim against my skin once again.

"Ready, my boy?" Travis finally asked when the uproarious and insistent conversation at lunch seemed to have finally petered out. One hundred people were talking at once, and at the same time listening in mild bewilderment to the strange sound of their own voices. There wasn't much to say, that was soon obvious. Yet we all went on talking, as if unwilling to face that conclusion. "All we've got to do," Travis said, as if reminding himself as we walked away from the crowd, "is remember what Goenka told us. The real test is out there. That's how we find out whether we've made any progress with this."

I was confident. I was high. There was no doubt about it. That morning, at the final session of *metta*, I had felt my love for the whole universe expand out of that room and go on forever. Whatever came next didn't seem to matter. "Rickshaw! Hey, wallah!" I called exuberantly to a driver of a three-wheeled pedaled taxi, as we stepped out through the little metal gate onto the street for the first time. A small, leathery, aged-looking man, although perhaps not much older than I, braked to a halt in front of us and sat on his bicycle seat mopping his brow with the rag that hung over one shoulder. Travis climbed on first and I got in after, telling the man where we wanted to go.

"Five rupees," he said, still wiping his sweat away.

"Don't be silly," I replied with a nervous laugh. "It's three from here."

"Five rupees." He didn't turn around. I could see his back through the holes in his shirt. His muscled legs dangled beside the pedals. I started to climb out, looking for another rickshaw, but my eyes couldn't seem to focus. Then all of a sudden I saw where I was. A blur of colored cloth, frantically struggling bodies, lurching machines, and obstinate animals dizzied me. I couldn't locate the street, and the gateway to the Burmese *vihara* looked like a keyhole. I would pay him ten rupees to get us out of there because I certainly couldn't move; my body felt like a sack of flour. Travis was yelling at him in broken Hindi. The man shouted back that we had plenty of money, he had none, so we could give him five rupees. Of course this was true but so was it true that the ride cost three rupees. The paradox nearly split my mind. I couldn't make distinctions like that. My eyes started to bulge. I had literally forgotten what to do. I had to do something. The rickshaw still wasn't moving. I couldn't close my eyes and watch my breath. Goenka, Hover, what should I do? "Travis," I croaked, "I'll pay him five rupees."

Travis shook his head, "Forget it, buying your way out doesn't pass the test either."

So we went for three, but paid dearly since the man's anger

was unbearable, numbing Travis and me into silence for the whole ride. The rest of the day went no better. It felt like I was stumbling around in someone else's dream. Choosing one size envelope over another at the post office was excruciating after weeks in which the greatest choice presented to me was between an orange and a banana for tea, and by a very simple process of alternation I'd long ago eliminated that confrontation.

The problem was more than choice. There was something indefinable in the air all around me, and as I sniffed it in bewilderment, it nearly knocked me out. Everything was moving strangely. We got out of our rickshaw right in the heart of the city, down near the Ganges River, the holiest spot in the world to Hindus, the place where they come to die. Here the banks of the river are lined with funeral pyres on the *ghats*, the steps leading to the river, creating an amazing festival of burning corpses. Holy men are as prevalent as street vendors. Behind the *ghats* are the narrow, winding sidestreets of the bazaar, packed with silk and brass merchants, tea stalls and restaurants.

As we wandered through this amazing scene of living, selling, and dying, I felt as ineffectual as a pin cushion. Every rude sound, every jostling body, every puzzling sight stuck in me. I had no mechanism left for comprehension—"Oh, I know what that is"—or even for dismissal of the unpleasant. I was gaping at everything.

I was helplessly aware. I couldn't be *more* removed from everything around me, but it was hardly a safe distance. I felt as if I would have to shout to be heard, to catch anyone's attention, to get anything done. And I didn't feel like shouting. I wanted to crawl into a hole. It wasn't intellectual revulsion. I had no sense of "Boy, what a foolish way to live. They should know what I know." Nothing looked familiar enough to judge. The impressions just kept floating through my head and spewing out like confetti. I felt like an interplanetary visitor, desperate to get back to his spaceship for a fix of canned air.

Travis and I stepped back onto the *vihara* grounds at dusk

and an involuntary sigh shook us both. A minute later, we were back in our tent munching a banana that tasted infinitely better than all the afternoon's restaurant food, which I'd spent forty days dreaming about. I looked at Travis's ashen face. His eyes were bloodshot. His hands trembled slightly. I was sure I looked worse.

"My boy," he finally said, "I guess this is what is called blown out."

"I don't understand it."

He shook his head angrily. "Goenka calls this an art of living? Forty days to develop equanimity and I was ready to kill that rickshaw driver."

"Which one?"

"I don't know, all of them!" The tent felt like it was going to explode. "I'm in great shape. And in twelve days I've got to be back in Canada. This is ridiculous. Look at me! I can't even walk out on the streets. When you met me I had a suntan, a healthy smile, and I loved meditating. Now I'm a basket case." Perhaps self-protectively I had ignored that transformation. He had experienced nothing as dramatic as my knots and fever. Just a very insistent and painful process of confronting himself each hour, each day, carefully peeling back the layers of defense. And tearing them free when they stuck. "I don't recognize what's left of me," he said with a little bitterness. "What blows me away out there is not *what* I'm watching . . ." He groped for words. "I'm not there. I'm out to lunch. My body's not there and neither is my mind. I'm scattered all over the place."

"So what are you going to do now?"

"Another course, quick, and hope I can put it all together before I have to get on the plane."

We were both silent. His decision to go on to Goenka's next retreat immediately meant that we'd part ways the day after next. I had hoped we could hang out together for a while before I left on my trip to Burma. It was very strange just then to think that I'd be going on alone. I kept thinking that somehow

Travis would materialize the money to come with me. I had forgotten by now what it was like not to be around him.

It had been a hard choice for me. Up until a week ago, our tentative plan had been for him to forget about the return portion of his excursion ticket back to Canada and to head down to Ceylon together on what money I had left. Then one day as I was sunning myself after lunch, I overheard a nearby conversation about a few people planning a trip to the International Meditation Center in Rangoon. I had spoken to some of those who had gone there in the fall with Hover and, though they really had little to say about their visit, there was something similar about all of them. A look in their eyes, as if they had seen something that no one else had. Now, apparently, there was a special occasion coming up at the Center, a memorial course commemorating the demise of U Ba Khin, the teacher of my teachers, which would be attended by all of his Burmese disciples. They were allowing some Western visitors to attend and I didn't know how, but I knew I would be one of them. Something about the sound of the place, maybe just the name, rung the same bell that went off the first time I'd heard "*Vipassana* Meditation" on the phone. Once again the decision was made, leaving only the details.

The hardest part was telling Travis. We had been keeping silence since Goenka's retreat, which began immediately following Hover's departure. Now I walked back into the tent and found him stretched out, sleeping or meditating, I wasn't sure. I was tempted to walk out. I knew that this was really going to interrupt things, but I couldn't sit with it for the next week.

"Well?" he said, opening his eyes.

"It looks like I'm on that trip to Burma."

He smiled, "I figured you would be."

"Really?" I answered in the tone of mock surprise I'd adopted from him.

"Sure, it seemed logical."

"And what about you?"

"Uh-uh." He exhaled and closed his eyes. "I don't want to

think about it." A short pause, then, "How much would it cost for me to go?" For a moment it was a wonderful possibility. The guy who had financed Travis' trip to India from the States was part of the contingent to Burma. We wondered if he could be persuaded. "Over a thousand dollars, including a new ticket back to Canada." Travis shrugged. "Too much to even ask."

Now, a week later, as we sat in the darkness of our tent, that decision was a little harder to live with. Travis got up and lit the candle, filling our space with a warm, comforting glow. I realized how much we had been able to take for granted together over these past weeks. I had never lived so easily with anyone before. It only now occurred to me that, despite the ego-wrenching experience we had both been through, and a physical proximity where there could be no masking, no hiding, I couldn't recall even a moment of hostility or resentment passing between us. Instead, there was cooperation and understanding. We wordlessly shared our food and cleaned each other's dishes. I had felt no competition with Travis, ever. Going through that same fire together had formed a bond of love and understanding.

We were silent the next morning during our ride to the train station and during most of the train ride to the city of Gaya. From there Travis would take a bus to the site of Goenka's next course a few hours away while I rode by rickshaw a few miles to nearby Bodh Gaya, the site of the Buddha's enlightenment and now a place of pilgrimage for Buddhists. I couldn't think about my stay there, nor my upcoming trip to Burma. My mind was stuck in a groove of dread over the sundering of our partnership. I couldn't even imagine this as anything but a joint venture. And Travis looked terrible. I probably did too, but he was the one I could see. Traveling all morning was just an extension of the previous day. It seemed almost dangerous that we should wander off separately now.

We embraced each other with pats on the back when it was time to go. "My boy," he said, "I have nothing to say."

I nodded. "Be happy."

"Yeah," he muttered. "I forgot about that."

And then I did what I was most afraid to do. I turned and walked out of the train station alone. And then there was a rickshaw and I was watching the incredible straining of those legs, this man's only commodity in life, drawing me through crowded city streets. I felt his momentary disappointment at each intersection, where he had to stop, relinquish his momentum, and begin all over the struggle to get his burden rolling. The air was full of the sweet, musky odor of Indian cigarettes mingled with rancid frying oil, cow dung, and human sweat. Something was missing though. My loneliness. Where was it? My friend the driver was chattering happily. In broken English he pointed out the sights. We'd left the outskirts of the city, and were rolling along a flat, tree-lined road. The sun was high and the air was warm. It would be nice if Travis were . . .

The thought died. A gentle breeze, maybe just the motion of the pedicab whiffed it away. I reached for it. It was gone. He was gone. And had taken loneliness with him. In a moment my mind was trapped in guilt. I should miss him. He was my friend. And then there was an eerie sensation of trying to recall what he looked like. And I couldn't. The bumps in the road clamored for my attention. And the crowds along the road as well. They were Tibetans. Refugees living now in India. Assembled here in this tiny shrine town to see their pope, the Dalai Lama. Esoteric Buddhist teachings. A sacred initiation called a *wong* was being staged here this week. A momentous occasion called the *Kali Chakra Wong*. I rolled these wonderful words around my tongue. Travis wanted to catch it. I tried to hold onto that thought. Loneliness would even be comforting now. Familiar in the face of this strange, unrecognizable feeling of floating adrift in the present.

Tents and encampments lined the road. Campfires everywhere. Seventy thousand pilgrims. Descendants of an ancient Buddhist tradition with a flavor of mystic mountains. The teaching blended with the culture it finds. Prayer beads clicking and mantra chanting rumbled in the air. I was giddy staring at processions of robed priests in strange headgear. Some with high peaks and others with duckbilled brims. Women with thick black braids and strings of turquoise and coral the size of pigeon's eggs hanging from their necks. Strange, rugged, placid faces reminded me of American Indian tribes. A unique vibration from them all, unlike any people I'd ever seen. I caught myself melting into it, a little guilty on my day of mourning. A little uneasy at how easy it was.

We stopped at the gateway to a walled enclosure. Another Burmese Buddhist *vihara*. Inside it was familiarly austere compared with the carnival in the streets. I recognized many faces. I marched through a swirl of details: arranging my accommodations for the next few days, discussing plans for the trip to Burma with my fellow travelers. And then I was alone again, lying on a wide-open grassy lawn. Was I numb? Was that it? Was that why I didn't feel anything? All I felt was the weight of my chest rising and falling with each breath. My memory was gone, that was all. And then I realized that this was the way it was supposed to be. This was what I'd been taught. It was as if after so many, many hours of staring with rooted attention at *this moment*, now, this pain, my mind had gotten locked into that position, unable to move from side to side, forward or back. And here I was, stuck gaping at the present, unable to remember, unable to plan.

The next day the streets were quieter. It was early morning. Bill, a friend from Benares, seemed to know just what was going on with my mind and body, so he held my hand, as it were, with a soothing string of not too meaningful conversation that had the effect of lulling me into a sense of familiarity.

The Bodhi Temple lay down a hill beneath the road. As we walked toward it, the hum of energy in the air increased in pitch. I could feel it. Bill explained that a few years before he had been deeply involved with Tibetan practice. At that time it was the only form of Buddhism in India. To me, its external trappings, visual symbolism, and ritual activity were entirely antithetical to the Buddha's simple teaching of the end of suffering through knowing reality. I looked at the elaborately carved medieval prismatic shape of the temple. I saw only a pile of rock. Everywhere devotees were bowing down full length on the ground over and over and over, as if doing calisthenics for football practice.

"Do they see Buddha as some sort of God?" I asked Bill.

"I suppose that on the popular level they do, and that's where most people's practice is. But, you know, it's no different in Burma or any of the other countries where Theravada, the supposedly pure teaching of Buddha is practiced. The real Tibetan teaching isn't worship at all, though. Even though they do the same prostrations and mantras, to those who are serious it means something very different. Just another way of confronting the ego."

I would have argued the point but we were at the temple now and the swirl of activity forced me to watch each step I made. I stopped and stared at a very old Tibetan man rhythmically bowing, kneeling, then fully prostrating before a statue of the Buddha. What did he want? What did he expect? It was confusing to me. It confronted some growing inner sense of mine of what this end of suffering was really all about. Not statues, not chanting. There's nothing out there! I felt like shouting it. Inside, inside. I wanted to turn around and head back to the peace of the *vihara*. Instead Bill led me by the arm around the temple, under strings of colored cloth prayer flags, through the whirring of the little prayer wheels, the revolving metal drums on sticks that the Tibetans carry.

He pointed to a tree surrounded by a heavy, carved stone railing and a curious mixture of reverent pilgrims and gawking sightseers. We stood off to the side. I wondered if I was supposed to say anything. Nice tree. Big deal. Its bark was dry and blotchy, its limbs kind of droopy. Like an old, retired man whiling away his empty time on a park bench. I was ready to leave. Instead, we sat down on a flat stone surface in a corner of the courtyard. I noticed after a moment that Bill's eyes were closed and his hands folded loosely in his lap. I did the same.

Almost immediately, that new-found sensor, which for lack

of better understanding I referred to as my "body," came alive. I felt a surge of power flowing through me. My back straightened up and my head and shoulders pulled into line. I felt my chest drawn forward in the direction of that tree. An enormous calm enveloped me. All the noise and humming and activity receded to a faint background whisper. I intuitively felt some inkling, some tiny hint of what had transpired in this spot twenty-five centuries ago. Was still going on. Right now. My mind rushed first for explanation, then for phrases of description like "vibrations" and "sanctified ground." But the words were babbling. I relaxed into awe. Place and time lost their meaning. *Where* I was experiencing this and *when* had no relevance.

My body told me it was so. It told me that the world can whir and hum and crank on with its noisy business, and yet the stillness is there. The peace is within. Prostrations and chanting and supplication and prayer clogged the air and yet that cool, empty space beneath that tree remained untouched. The Buddha still sat there, as he did twenty-five hundred years ago, with eyes closed and attention turned inward. And even though he was alone then, in silence, still the outside world confronted him. His own desires for that world, his senses, and the machinery of his mind assaulted him with a thousand prostrations and supplications and prayers for his attention. And he continued to turn inward, deeper and deeper within.

I was just on the edge, the most distant approach to that space within, standing before an unknown universe of infinite possibility. To go further I could carry nothing with me, no baggage of the outer world. These past weeks had been a reluctant, painful process of giving up that baggage. But I'd done it. And so forfeited my right to travel out there. I would be blown out if I tried. That kind of tourism was dead for me.

We seemed to open our eyes together. I shook my head slowly in amazement. Few words came out. As my mind started rolling again, though, it wanted to know . . . how, what had I felt? Where had I been? Bill shrugged. "This is a pretty amazing place. Actually the whole town is like this usually, but now you can hardly notice it underneath all of this activity." Then he smiled. "Wait until you go to the Meditation Center in Rangoon. That's a pretty amazing space too. The meditation cells where U Ba Khin taught . . . it reminds me of this place."

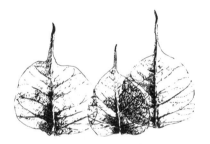

7

No Way Off This Path

Six of us arrived at the International Meditation Center in Rangoon late in the afternoon of the day the retreat in memory of U Ba Khin was to begin. A charming, middle-aged Burmese gentleman who produced movies for a living met us at the gate and immediately took us on a tour of the grounds. After all the build-up and expectation that had surrounded our trip it was difficult to appreciate the fact that we were actually there. All we could do was gawk as we followed our host around. The most prominent feature of the Center was the arrangement of the meditation cells, the small individual rooms where one was expected to sit in darkness and silence for most of the day. They surrounded a large central pagoda that contained the shrine room where U Ba Khin himself had sat in meditation. Opening onto the shrine room were eight cells, which were also accessible by doors from the outside. In the shrine room there was a large marble statue of the Buddha and a flower-decked photograph of U Ba Khin, seated in profile. Our host detailed the history of the Center as we stood in silence on the parquet floor in our bare feet, staring at the picture of the master. I didn't catch most of what was said. My attention was fixed on the photo. The man in it seemed to be enormous, though the Burmese are normally small. He had a powerful, almost bulldoggish head and neck, and did not look at all like your retiring recluse.

Outside, the pagoda was surrounded by a circular deck with little stone benches and huge pots of tropical plants and flowery viny bushes everywhere. *Sayagyi* ("The Great Teacher"), our host remarked, had taken a very special interest in the gardening around the Center. Next to the pagoda was a large screen-enclosed hall where the teacher had discoursed. When you entered, your attention was drawn immediately to the chair where he sat. It seemed overly large, almost surreal. Behind it hung an enormous picture of the teacher himself. Next to his chair was a smaller chair, which, we were told, was where Sayama had sat. I wasn't quite sure of the role she played then or now. Her title of "assistant" didn't give me much of a picture. I asked if she also taught meditation. "Surely," our host replied, but in a way that said I hadn't asked the right question yet.

Finally we were shown our rooms, lovely little bungalows with large screened windows, looking out on lush green hills. Then, after we were given bedding and mosquito nets, our host excused himself for a while, leaving us on our own to wander about.

A thick layer of quietness hung over the entire place, but I wasn't really sure of its nature. My first impression was actually of a sense of ghostliness. The reminders of U Ba Khin were everywhere, but all I felt was his absence. The museumlike atmosphere was disappointing. One of the others in our group commented that he recognized the feeling from other ashrams he'd visited after the guru's demise. When I suddenly looked up at the whole place from the dining hall down the hill, it seemed to me more like a summer camp in New England than a place for the grand psychic adventure I had anticipated.

When we had let it be known that we were coming to this Center, the six of us had been given all sorts of hints and enigmatic descriptions about the place and particularly about Sayama, the woman who had been U Ba Khin's leading disciple and was now the major force in charge of the place. She was supposed to have certain psychic powers, the nature of which was never spelled out. In Calcutta, in between running around for our visas and airline tickets, we had spent a lot of time shopping for appropriate gifts for the woman who, we were told, liked dress material and fine woolen sweaters. She'll probably greet you wearing fancy jewelry and makeup, we were warned. The picture of a fashionable, Burmese mystic mother was hard to conjure up. Now that we were actually at the Center, we nervously awaited her arrival, each one of us wondering, I'm sure, whether we would go through with the planned formality of prostrating at her feet as we were told was proper.

An old, round-body, British-make automobile pulled into the driveway and a number of Burmese got out. There were several women in the group, so we had to decide quickly at whose feet to dive. A woman of about fifty, carrying packages in her arms and looking as if she was on her way to the kitchen to get dinner ready in a hurry, stopped in front of us for a moment, scanned our eyes, broke into a little chuckle, and then was off on her business. We had missed our chance to prostrate before Sayama.

I had a hard time believing any of it. The meditation teachers whom we were introduced to looked mostly like middle-class, well-fed civil servants, which in fact, they were. During his life, U Ba Khin was the Accountant General of the national government, and a great many of his disciples were people who worked in his department. The whole gathering seemed more like a social club outing than a meditation retreat, with old friends and their wives embracing, exchanging news of their families, and lugging suitcases and bedding.

I wasn't much heartened when eventually all of us took our

places in the cells surrounding the central shrine room to receive our instructions and begin *vipassana* meditation. The cell doors were open so that we faced Sayama and her husband, U Chit Tin, the organizer of activities, who sat beside her on the wooden floor. A small, round man, U Chit Tin was one of U Ba Khin's oldest disciples. One day, many years ago, he had brought his wife Sayama to the Center for instruction. U Ba Khin had immediately recognized her spiritual abilities, and after a period of training, Sayama had become his assistant. She and U Chit Tin virtually moved into the Center and she played an integral role in U Ba Khin's teaching.

Sayama spoke no English, so U Chit Tin translated as she half-chanted, half-spoke instructions to us in a soft, breathy voice. It all seemed pretty slack and made me anxious to get back to my own cell downstairs and at least do some serious meditation. After having us repeat the precepts of conduct and giving us our meditation instructions, Sayama said something to U Chit Tin, who told us to direct our attention to the top of our heads. I did, and it felt as though someone had dropped a brick on me. My entire body was immediately filled with a burning sensation as if a hole had been drilled at the very top of my head and hot liquid was being poured in. And for the next half hour I sat there in incredible pain as I sensed an almost magnetic pull from that shrine room.

It was now very apparent to all of the visitors that besides this casual older couple and their friends tending the relics of a dead teacher, there was something important about this place. Powerful was the only word we could come up with. There was literally something I could feel in my body, now that Sayama had made me aware of it, almost a constant background presence. My body registered it as if the air itself here was humming, vibrating all the time. My body was more alive, as if it were a sensor combining seeing and hearing.

This phenomenon became most intense when I entered my individual meditation cell, a dark, wooden-floored cubicle large enough to stand and lie down in, about four feet wide, with a door that bolted closed from the inside, sealing off all light. All of our meditation took place in those individual cells, whose power began to have a certain awe for me. At seven different hours a day I entered my cell and the click of the bolt was like flipping the dial on some psychic washing machine. My mind and body were somehow being cleansed.

The process created a strange addiction. Now that I, and my companions as well, recognized the power of this place, though we certainly could not explain it, our planned visits of two one-week stays here, interrupted by a necessary trip to Bangkok to renew our visas, seemed absurdly brief. This looked like a unique opportunity to go deeper into this meditation than I'd ever considered. Each hour became precious to us all. I would return to my cell with the hungry expectation of a lover or a junkie. Early morning and late evening all of us spent extra hours meditating, beyond what the teachers prescribed. It felt to all of us that our minds were being slowly roasted. But with only fourteen days available, we wanted to throw dynamite into the fire. A loud, clanging, insistent bell called us back from our inner worlds at eleven each day for lunch, the second and last meal of the day. Increasingly I was having more trouble making the transition from one side of my cell door to the other. Not just because I felt the preciousness of the available time, but because I was having a hard time dragging my attention outward from the mind-blowing drama of watching my organism unraveling. Outside my meditation cell I felt raw, exposed. I would have preferred to rest quietly before returning, but clearly my hosts had a very different style. One morning as I emerged for lunch and was standing in the sunlight, letting my eyes slowly adjust, I was startled by the sound of a tricycle bell. I don't know the Burmese for "Look out!" If I did, the five-year-old boy, Sayama's grandson, would not have run over my foot with his speeding vehicle. My jaw dangled. Who, what, how could they let him . . . Suddenly I flashed to U Chit Tin's last whispered word to us as we left the Center for a day in Bangkok to get our visas renewed. I was all seriousness, expecting transcendent wisdom from him to guide us in our dealings with the world outside. He, too, was serious. "Don't forget," he exhorted us, "to get some chocolate bars for the little boy on your way back."

I watched the boy park his tricycle, carefully following his grandmother's admonitions to avoid the flower beds. The Burmese were bustling about, showering, hanging clothes to dry, and getting ready for lunch. My other companions, the five other Westerners, emerged from their cells like groundhogs in winter. When U Chit Tin came by to round us up, I told him about the traffic collison. He laughed, and I commented on the importance of Noble Silence.

"Yes, yes," he nodded emphatically, "that is very true. But you know," and he looked at me with what I'd come to recognize as his important smile, "we don't like the long faces here. People taking themselves so seriously, walking around with heads down. That is not the way to practice."

At five o'clock each day we gathered outside the discourse hall, where we drank a fruit juice concoction that Sayama prepared for us. One evening, as I sat on the concrete bench outside the discourse hall sipping juice, I could feel the collective exhaustion of my companions. U Chit Tin and a few other Burmese joined us, interrupting our intense silence with cheerful inquiries about the suitability of the accommodations, the well-being of Goenka and Hover, and news of their other pupils abroad. It was difficult for me to focus on the words and more difficult for me to understand why I had to. I couldn't politely remind U Chit Tin and the others that silence was the best policy. I rationalized conversing with them as a small way of repaying the exquisite care and attention they were lavishing upon us. Meanwhile, my jaw felt rubbery just from talking. Finally it was time for us all to go inside to gather around the long wooden table at the back of the discourse hall for our meeting with the teachers. During this meeting, we reported our experiences and they commented.

Sayama sat at the far end with U Chit Tin beside her. Near-by was Goenka's brother, Babulal, a smaller version of the Indian teacher, whose remarkable resemblance to his brother always caught us by surprise. Also there was U Ba Pho, the slightly elegant cigarette-smoking secretary of the Vipassana Association, a warmly eloquent man who delighted in reciting stories of the old days at the Center. There was also a man named U Tint Yee, who was referred to as the chairman of the Association, which meant that, at least in title, he was U Ba Khin's successor.

At first it wasn't apparent why U Tint Yee held that position. Unlike the others, he seemed almost shy in our presence, keeping his eyes down and initially not conversing much. He also seemed a little more austere than the rest. He was thin and angular with a broad face that narrowed to a sharply pointed chin; slightly bucktoothed with pursed lips. I noticed, though, that he often replied to our questions without Sayama speaking first. And when he did the other teachers listened respectfully.

The five other Westerners and I sat around the table fidgeting and uneasy. Sayama pointed at us one by one and we told her what had happened in our cells that day. When it came around to one of the more humorous members of our entourage, he threw up his hands and remarked that the afternoon was three hours of wandering thoughts interrupted every now and then by his breath. Then he dropped his joking manner and leaned forward at the table. He was angry. "What can I do with my mind? I can't concentrate. My thoughts won't stop long enough!"

U Tint Yee sat up straight in his chair. The muscles of his high cheeks flexed as he phrased his reply. "What your mind does," he said slowly, in a gentle but unwavering tone, as if he were trying to toss the words perfectly past all the obstacles of our comprehension, "What your mind does, is not your business." We were all silent. He continued, "What you are doing now is watching the breath and the sensations within the body. That is all. Once you become aware that your mind has wandered and that you're somewhere else, then return to your breathing again. Don't think about the thought, don't react to the fact that you weren't attentive a moment ago. At this instant, now, you are aware, so place that awareness on the breath. Again and again and again. Right now. To become agitated that you forgot about your breath is letting the awareness go to the past. This meditation is watching what is going on right here and now. Noting that you have not been doing it for two minutes or a whole hour is still not doing it."

U Tint Yee waited and stared at us, watching to see if the words had penetrated. He saw all of us wrestling with his words just the way we wrestled with our minds in those cells. Then, as if to demonstrate, his entire face and body relaxed, visibly. "You see," he said. "You can't strain to be attentive." And then he paused, as if waiting for the right phrase to come to him. "It must be an attitude of zestful ease. And if the mind is agitated, then stop, get up and walk around. When you are calmer, then start again."

I couldn't stop staring at U Tint Yee. His erect, relaxed posture, his shy, warm smile, and his deep, steady, brown eyes were talking to me. Meditation has nothing to do with words. Yet at certain key moments, the words and the experience coalesce and the understanding of the process takes a leap to a place that all the words in the world couldn't have described a moment before.

Perhaps I'd heard what U Tint Yee had to say many times before from other teachers, but right then I saw it. I saw him. The teacher and the teaching became one. And I understood "zestful ease". And then I immediately saw much more, everything I'd been exposed to from the minute I'd arrived there: the elaborate meals, the casual conversation, the shouting grandchildren. *Don't take yourself so seriously*. A strange teaching. This meditation is not about doing anything. Zestful ease. Not doing. Not doing nothing either. Alertness. Awareness.

I returned to my cell and the struggle was over. Sitting was no longer a problem. Something had happened, I'll never really *know* what it was. My being had altered in a way I could never have foreseen. I knew, intuitively, that some barrier, a resistance, had been overcome. I was sitting there and there was no difficulty, no fight, no desire not to be sitting. *What your mind does is not your concern.* And he was absolutely right. Suddenly the strange, powerful, violent, or frightening gestures of my mind were no problem. I had another concern. Being alert, aware.

I was hooked. I knew it. The experiment was over. I'd never get off this train, no matter if I tried. Resolve was no longer keeping me on, but rather something beyond my comprehension. I settled back for the ride.

Lunch was the meal we were always expected promptly for, and no wonder. The two cooks under Sayama's supervision lavished so much attention on the preparation of the meal, perhaps the most subtly flavored food I've ever tasted, that we were absolutely obliged to snap out of our internal dramas and partake in the group ceremony of mealtime. It was a strange ceremony. Usually we entered the cool, shaded eating hall in silence, seating ourselves on the woven mats about the low, round wooden table set aside for our visiting group. We were always thankful for the shade and cool breeze that blew in across the screened veranda. The Burmese participants were at a couple of other tables with the one next to ours occupied by Sayama, U Chit Tin, U Tint Yee, and several other teachers whose arrival as a group signalled the end of silence. Sayama was the master of ceremonies, shouting orders for the serving of the meal and pointedly taking in our reactions to the food. She chuckled contentedly at our amazed enjoyment of the delicate clear soups, sparkling rice, and endless vegetable dishes, usually followed by platters of tropical fruit.

The first bites were the hardest. As I lifted the porcelain spoon from my soup bowl, I felt as though I was plumbing ocean depths. Then I heard Sayama's animated voice in the midst of some story at the other table that ended with side-splitting laughter from her companions. The energy in the dining hall was like a slow eddy that becomes a whirlpool. The food, the table, the laughter, the people made me want to flee back to my cell. Everything spun faster and faster until everyone got up and the room emptied and I was flung out on the lawn under a tree, dazed. U Chit Tin came over.

"The books that you all wanted on Buddhism will be here tomorrow. Day after that is the last day. Perhaps we'll go to the market downtown in the morning before the plane leaves. That might be nice."

U Ba Pho, joined us. "Did you enjoy lunch?" he inquired. I nodded. Of course I did. It was magnificent. But I wasn't here to eat. I was here to get . . . to be . . .

Perhaps U Ba Pho saw the question in my eyes. "Yes," he said, "it is such excellent food Sayama prepared for us. But you know, it is so good only to here," and he brought the flat of his palm to his throat. "And then?" He laughed. "What is it then? *Anicca*, only that."

The next step. The next step. It was clear now where I wanted to go. My goal was clear. I could do what must be done. But how? Vaguely I made plans to return here in the spring. Aside from that my itinerary was a blank. I wanted to go to Ceylon, to live for awhile in a house or maybe even in a Buddhist monastery. None of the group I was travelling with was interested in accompanying me. They were all returning to India to be with Goenka. For some reason that didn't appeal to me. There was something else to do, but I didn't know what.

Finally I asked U Chit Tin what would be best. It seemed I could either live somewhere in a house, maybe with some people, sitting part of the day, working the rest, maybe writing some, or continue this intensive schedule. What did he think? He nodded, as if the question had a yes or no reply. "Go slowly," he smiled, telling me, I thought, to head for my comfortable house on the beach, "and do a thirty-day course."

How to decide? That seemed more crucial than what to decide.

One morning at breakfast during my first week at the

Center, it had occurred to me that I might shave off the bushy brown and red beard that had covered my face for the past five years. I considered how it might look, how others might perceive it. I could always grow it back, I decided. Then when I went to sit, I tabled the debate and began watching my breath. But as I sat there in the dark, a strange feeling welled up from my belly. It was an impulse and urge to act that wasn't working through my mind or even my emotions. The beard should go. My mind got the message and accepted the command. Okay, I would do it in a couple of days. End of discussion. Back to meditation. My body rumbled, *Do it now!* I nearly opened my eyes in fright. Who said that? My mind hadn't, yet I heard the message, as if my body had spoken. Okay, okay, my mind replied, right after lunch. Clean as a whistle. *NOW!* was the reply. I shook with fear and struggled to keep my body from walking right out of the cell then and there. Lunchtime arrived, and I let my mind's reasonable hold go and watched in amazement as my body took over complete control, marched into the washroom, and left me staring in the mirror at a totally unfamiliar, clean-shaven face.

Now it was almost time to leave Burma, clean-shaven face and all. I sat in my cell wrestling with the possible courses of action, all the time knowing that it was a futile process. The hour vow ended. I lay down in my cell, relaxed, and spread my attention out in my body, comforted by the sensation of everything dissolving, reassuring me that I wasn't really there. My mind could no longer decide anything, that was clear. But still the need for action remained. I was not prepared to just let things happen. I didn't believe that that kind of randomness served the purpose of the path and the goal. No, I would have to act. Every minute I would have to act. But I could no longer use my mind to tell me what to do.

I felt my whole being sinking into my belly. I felt the possibilities rumble there. My breath seemed to stop and the cell was absolutely quiet. I was listening in silence. And then I heard my body speak. *Go to Ceylon: go alone.*

8

Unmeasured Time

THE ENTIRE ISLAND OF Ceylon
has only eight million inhabitants, and as I stood idly waiting
for a bus or walked through the streets of Colombo, the capital
city, I no longer felt the constant psychic assault that I had been
aware of in India. The most obvious difference, however, was
that Ceylon was a Buddhist country. Even the most casual conversation easily turned to a common appreciation of the *Dharma*. There are probably no more Ceylonese who actually
practice the heart of Buddha's teachings than there are real
practitioners of any religion anywhere, but everyone I met at
least understood the value of his teachings and was willing to
support those who really did wish to pursue them.

The bus that took me out of Colombo was steamy hot.
Uncomplaining people packed against each other, creating a
vibrant heat, and intermittent rain kept the windows shut. Since
my clothes were soaked with sweat anyway, I would have
taken the rain over the heat. At least I had a seat, reserved for

the clergy. This seemed appropriate, since I was on my way to check into a Buddhist monastery.

It was nearly dark when the driver stopped the bus at a crossroads between two towns and pointed up a hill to the left. I got out, and he handed me my bag, wishing me good luck. A minute later with my bag slung over my back like a pack, I set off on the dirt road.

The trip hadn't been easy. Since my departure from Burma some two weeks ago, I'd traveled alone in a space of portable solitude. There'd been sickness in India, a difficult moment of parting from my friends back in Calcutta, and, now that my money had begun to evaporate, long journeys on cheap trains. All along this winding path from Calcutta to Ceylon I'd had endless choices, endless routes to take, but at each crossroads the right trail was marked perfectly clearly, if only to my eyes.

On the way south to Ceylon I had stopped in Pondicherry, an odd city on the southeast coast of India once ruled by the French, to visit my cousin Rose, who had been in India for some time now as a member of a pioneer utopian-type community known as Auroville, an offshoot of the ashram founded by Sri Aurobindo. The members of the community lived in beautiful thatched houses with poured concrete floors. Fresh tropical fruit, whole wheat bread, cow's milk, nuts, and vegetables were their diet. Farming, building, and planning were their way of life. I spent about three days with my cousin Rose, following her around as she showed me other parts of the sprawling community. Amazing modern structures of concrete and steel rising up out of semidesert, beautiful two-story homes by the beach. Artists at work, small schools. I listened to her own plans to build a new house and plant cash crops.

One afternoon Rose and I went for a long walk to the beach to visit some friends. Rose wasn't perfectly happy with the home she had, and one of the reasons she took me to see her friends was that their dwelling was a model for what she wanted. "Isn't it nice?" she kept asking me, unsure herself and worried about where the money to build a new house might come from. She accepted my silence perhaps as tacit approval. I was glad she didn't insist; I didn't know if I would be able to lie or to explain just what I felt. Of course it's nice, I would have wanted to say, but nice doesn't matter. But how could I explain that "doesn't matter" was simply a verbal approximation of my reaction at that moment to those surroundings. The locus of reality had drawn so close to me that I could no longer even dare to say, "that over there is nice." The event, the actuality of what was happening right then, was not in this house, these surroundings. Reality was going on right inside me. The only event was my mind's reaction to whatever was around me.

What made me so sure of this? In those long, open-ended hours in the cell the evidence had become overwhelming that it was not what was out there, not even people, that made me suffer, made me glad. It was my mind. And my mind was not something I seemed to have any control over. Something automatic took place, like thunder after lightning. When I looked at the house Rose showed me, my mind's reaction sent my whole being into elation or disgust or boredom or depression or the zillion other variations that we call being alive. And that's why what happens *out there* assumes such huge importance. Because when there is no control over the automatic reaction, then the only thing to do is pick certain reactions that at least for a time are more comfortable, less painful. That becomes pleasure. But that pleasure is dependent on something out there happening a certain way so that the automatic reaction will register pleasure. When one of the women Rose lived with told me that after a time I'd be back there, too, since there was no better place to live, I smiled. Paradise wasn't what I was seeking, but I was glad I had stopped in to find that out. My cousin and her friends couldn't understand my rush to be on. I didn't either. But I knew that this was not what I was looking for and that right then my attention seemed to be diving inward, seeking the source, the wellspring of the conditioning of my mind. There was nothing out there that I was willing to turn my attention to.

It was a very different way of being that my life had evolved into. The life I had so recently led was based on thought and decision, and the rationale that preceded decision arose from a process that seemed unreliable to me now. I no longer trusted my thoughts, because they weren't me. The only thing recognizable enough for me to rely on now was an unspoken intuition about the very next move. Not its implications, its ramifications, or the results it would produce, but simply what I ought to do next.

Now I was in Ceylon on my way to a monastery. I walked to the crest of a hill and looked out across a long, lush valley of cultivated fields. At the top of the far hill I saw the spire of the pagoda.

I reached the top of the hill and hastened down the other side into the rapidly darkening valley. It looked like I had a good walk ahead of me. The rain was starting up again and my clothes were pretty wet, but that was all right. The valley was one of the most beautiful places I'd ever been anywhere in the world. It was a remarkable balance between human cultivation and the earth's desire to keep itself so thickly covered by vegetation that it would be protected from disturbances by man. So it appeared that the large tracts of rice fields and vegetable gardens were just on loan while the abutting forests waited impatiently to reclaim their own. There was a vibrant energy to this land unlike most of what I'd seen in India, where the earth had been beaten into submission for so many thousands of years that nothing grew there now without a struggle. In Ceylon there was an easiness, a spontaneity to growth. The sun didn't set this close to the equator, it crashed, and the colors of purple evening hanging over the emerald fields were electric. Brown trails marked the edges of the fields, and wild flowers dotted the entire scene with hot hues of red and orange.

A loinclothed farmer leaned on his hoe and smiled as I came up to him.

"*Aranya?*" I asked pointing up the hill. It was the old Buddhist word for a forest hermitage, I'd been told.

"*Aranya, aranya,*" he nodded, happily gesturing onward.

At the foot of the hill a neat stone stairway marked the entrance to the monastery. When I got to the top, I stood at the edge of a large, open courtyard, catching my breath and looking at a group of monks waiting for me at the far end. Suddenly I felt unsure about just how my request to stay and meditate would be received. What if they refused? There were no buses back to Colombo tonight. Only one other Westerner had ever stayed here for any length of time, and the American anthropologist who had told me about this place had not exactly been encouraging when I decided to come. I started preparing a number of introductory lines, all of which seemed to be amazingly long tangles of words. I could see their faces staring at me as I approached. They were smiling, and it occurred to me that I must look like a drowned rat. Were they smiling at my appearance? Almost before I realized it, I found myself facing an old, baby-faced monk on the porch of a small cottage. He was apparently the head monk. I dropped my bags, fell to my knees, and prostrated before him as he intoned his blessings in a somber but loving voice. When I looked up I saw a twinkle in his eyes, and I had the amazing sensation that he had been waiting there for me in that seat and was saying, "Wonderful, you've finally arrived." He didn't speak a word of English, but a layman who was standing beside him spoke enough for me to let him know that I wished to stay here and do solitary meditation. As the news spread among the group of monks standing there, everyone seemed to be delighted. Then after a while, an English-speaking monk was summoned from some far corner of the monastery. When the short, smiling, shy monk arrived, what everyone had already grasped was formalized into words.

While others asked me how I'd gotten there, Nyayaka Maha Thera, as the head monk was known, like a doting grandfather saw to it that I got out of my wet clothes, had a proper bath, and was fed. When all this was accomplished, our translator, a *bhikku*, or monk named Sunno, described the layout of the place. Spreading out from the central courtyard into the hills in all directions were numerous *kutis*, little cottages where one could live in varying degrees of seclusion. There were caves up on the cliffs, especially prepared for retreats. Maha Thera barked orders to the younger monks, some of whom looked no more than twelve, to get keys and lamps and collect some furniture. There was one place in particular that would be good for me, he said. It was a hut in the forest all alone with a stream below it way on the other side of the hill. Unfortunately it was occupied by a local school official who was here for a few days. Until he left I could have the *kuti* where the anthropologist usually stayed, which was built into the rock at the top of a hill overlooking the monastery.

The two monks led the way with lamps across the now-dark courtyard and up long flights of rock steps till we arrived at a cleared verandalike area at the entrance to two caves. Natural rock formations had transformed them into little huts. Huge overhanging stones served as roof and rear wall. Plaster and stone formed the front wall, which had a door and windows. The inside of the cave was smoothed over with plaster and whitewash. It was furnished with a little table, a chair, and a low rope bed with a mattress on which I spent an enormously restful night until I was awakened by the gong that roused the community at four in the morning.

Just after sunrise, I bathed in a spring-fed pool located conveniently in a deep niche in the rock just beside my *kuti*, and then stepped out onto the wide terrace overlooking the whole monastery. The structures of the monastery were built into and around the existing rock formations so that even trees were left undisturbed. The cliffs were used as a natural buffer to whatever civilization was nearby. Looking down I saw yellow-robed men intently sweeping their walkways with delicate brooms, while others busily gathered flowers for ceremonial offerings from lush, tended gardens. The day's work had commenced on a new teaching and instruction hall that was being built on the hill beneath the main courtyard. The work was personally overseen by Maha Thera himself. As I descended the hill, I felt as if I was in some elfin workshop. Huts dotted the hill, housing monks busy at work or study, and chanting floated out of open windows. I caught a few smiles but no one approached me with conversation. When I reached the inner court where the monks were fed, I was directed to a corner room. There I sat alone at a small low table and feasted on delicious rice cakes mixed with milk, noodle pancakes, chutney, fruit, and coconut sweets with tea, the offerings of the lay people for the hermitage's inhabitants, all in quantities I couldn't hope to eat. This was how all my meals would be served, apart from the monks. I would be left entirely on my own. From the end of the noon meal until seven the next morning I would be all to myself in that small cave at the top of the hill.

One day at six in the evening there was a knock at the door of my cave. At first I didn't respond. Then I remembered what it signified. Maha Thera was requesting my presence. I followed two young monks down the hill and back to the end of the courtyard to the little porch where Maha Thera had sat on the evening of my arrival and where he sat every morning for all the monks to receive his blessings and well-wishing. That was one ceremony I took part in. This evening when, answering his summons, I prostrated before him, his smile seemed more gleeful than usual, even a little playful. Pointing to the red and white checkered *lungi* that I wore wrapped around my waist, and my purple T-shirt, he shook his head. I didn't think I was that inappropriately dressed, but he had other ideas. With a dramatic flourish, he signaled to one of the younger monks, who handed me an old, neatly folded yellow *lungi* and a yellow-dyed shirt. Maha Thera motioned for me to go inside and put them on, and when I reappeared he clapped his hands together and called several other monks to come over and see what he had produced. It wasn't full monk's garb, but the uniform for a layman living at the monastery. Quite pleased, Maha Thera sent me back to my dwelling.

After dark I heard a lot of noise in the courtyard, and when I finally went out to see what was going on, the walkways below were lit up by rows of burning candles on long poles. Lights were on in the main hall and I heard chanting. The next morning when I walked down the hill to breakfast, I found the monastery filled with crowds of visiting laymen. The young man who had so graciously served me my meals was going to be ordained. My first impulse after three days alone in my cave was to run inside and bolt the door. But soon I was sitting in the large, cool, marble-floored hall among the friends and family of the young monk-to-be, facing Maha Thera and four or five senior monks as they chanted their way through the ceremony. The ritual was austere but impressive. It was a rite of passage, the journey from one world to another. The young man left the hall dressed as I had been before Maha Thera had given me my new clothes. He returned with his head shaved, dressed in yellow-draped robes identical to those of all his brothers and so distinct from the clothes of those in the audience. Gone forth, from home to homelessness, is what the ceremony is called. The going forth. I looked around quickly at those who'd come to bid him good-bye from their world. I tried to gauge their reaction, but it wasn't visible. All I could think was that my mother would be appalled, and in some way I was, too, almost automatically. I was aware of the attitude toward monks of any sort that I had been brought up with, even my particular culture's attitude toward celibate Catholic priests. Something strange, unnatural about it; a man has got to be somewhat, well . . . have some sort of problem to want to live without a woman all his life, to want to live within walls. That was the picture. Walls were an escape, and a monk was somehow less than a man, someone who couldn't handle all of life. I smiled now at the lie. The young man's rite of passage was not a flight but a conscious evolution.

One of the older monks began to speak in Singhalese. A layman sitting beside me explained that it was a lecture on the virtues of monastic life. I didn't get much more of a translation, so I got up quietly and left.

Outside there was a crowd of some sixty or seventy of the

monastery's residents who had assembled for the ceremony. The beauty of their clear, shining faces was dazzling. There were some who had spent nearly their entire lives behind these walls and yet their faces showed no signs of deprivation. Others, young men in their twenties with the grace of swans, bore on their faces expressions of absolute unconcern. Assurance was molded into their being. All lived by endless rules in here. All had to dress the same way, eat the same thing at the same time with the same kind of bowl, perform the same rituals, rise at the same hour, with absolutely no freedom except for the mind.

Suddenly there was a tap on my shoulder. It was *bhikku* Sunno, who had translated for me on my arrival. He himself had only been here for a little more than six months. Before that he had worked as an engineer in London, living the life most Ceylonese only dream about. Now he talked to me enthusiastically about his new life here. With a small group of fellow practitioners he lived separate from the rest of the monks in the meditation section of the monastery, a self-enclosed community designed to provide even greater seclusion from distraction to those engaged in full-time meditation. I was surprised when he said that he only practiced meditation a few hours a day. When I told him about the kind of schedule I had been taught, he nodded pleasantly. "There is time for that," he said, "but now I am just getting used to the life here, and starting slowly. We have all the time in the world here, you know." He smiled. "This place gives you every opportunity for the practice."

"It's nice, isn't it?" I turned in the direction of the squeaky voice to face an old, elflike monk. With a mischievous smile, he grabbed my hand, grandly brushed off my palm, nodded with a jerk over his shoulder at the ordination ceremony, then looked back at my palm. "Your time isn't that far off." I could easily believe him. Although it seemed amazing, considering what my whole life had been, right now I felt the strongest pull in the direction of this monastic life.

When I returned to my cave in midmorning, I was totally exhausted. Just talking with the monks had suddenly called up unused muscles that now cramped. I appreciated the experience of the monks; it gave me a clearer picture of the activities of the wider monastery: its relation to the community of lay people around it, and its function, not only as a meditation center but as a school for young monks. My proximity to all of this, however, lessened the solitude that I wanted. The next morning I mentioned once more to Sunno about the hut in the forest I'd been told of on my arrival. He promised me to speak again to Maha Thera, but another day or two went by and still no one approached me. Finally on the afternoon of the fifth day, instead of remaining in my cave as usual at teatime, I went down to the courtyard. Maha Thera was surprised to see me and the serious expression on his face became a giggle. Then, closing his eyes and folding his hands he made a serious face of mock meditation, and asked me, without words, how it was all going. With some of the Pali words I knew I told him it was going so well I wanted to move to the *kuti* in the forest. "Ahhh, yes," his face expressed, then he sent for Sunno for a more literal translation.

When Sunno arrived I apologized to him for dragging him from his meditation. "It's quite all right," he politely replied, then listened, chewing thoughtfully on his lower lip as Maha Thera spoke. Apparently the old head monk felt that my move to the forest was a formidable step and he wanted to make sure I was ready for it, which is why he had waited for me to come to him. In fact, I had to insist on going and make it clear that I would walk over there by myself if no one would take me. When Maha Thera was finally convinced that my decision to go was absolute, he sent a young monk to get the keys. Meanwhile I returned to my cave, packed up my things, and reappeared on the porch. Incredibly enough I had to go through the whole routine of asking him all over again before he sent the young monk to lead me to my new home. We walked up a large hill at the rear of the courtyard where the dining hall was and then along a ridge passing two or three other *kutis* where some old monks lived in relative solitude. Then we followed a long path down into a slight clearing, maybe fifty feet square, in the middle of which sat a stone and plaster hut, with a pitched roof of Spanish-style clay tiles. Inside the white walls it was cool and dark. The single spacious room contained two beds on opposite walls, a good-sized table, and chair. The smoothness of the stone floors and the craftmanship on the wooden windows lent an air of precision rather than rusticity. The young monk showed me the path that led down to the stream, the toilet in the rear of the building, how to work the lamp, and every other detail he thought I would need to know.

As soon as the monk left, I set to work sweeping the floor, putting a cloth over the table and setting out my books, laying out the contents of my bag just so on the spare bed, and selecting the proper pillow to sit on for my meditation. When all this was done, the next logical thing to do, it seemed, was to sit, and so after closing the door and the windows, I made myself comfortable atop the bed and closed my eyes. Within a few minutes, I felt the darkness outside blow in like a storm. I could even hear it. In a single instant, as if a curtain had been raised on a new act, the woods were alive with a whole new set of sounds. The sharp chirping of crickets formed a melodious backdrop to the sudden, violent, crashing sounds of unidentifiable creatures making their way through the night forest that surrounded the clearing on all sides. The screams of monkeys crashing through the trees made me shudder, and the hooting of birds seemed directed right at me. I couldn't distinguish what was inside and what was outside. A scurrying sound which seemed to be right on the floor in front of me, or even on the bed, caused me to open my eyes. I would look up and shine my flashlight all around the room. I felt like a helpless victim. Human beings were not in control here. In the chaotic free play of nature, I felt as powerful as an insect. Suddenly walls as a form of protection, as something to shut out all that, seemed desperately important to me. I felt fear well up in my chest. Not simply fear to hide, but the fear that wanted to crush all that activity outside in order to control it. I watched my mind swirl into fantasies of violent death until I leaped up from the bed, ran to the door, and threw it open. It was so dark outside I couldn't see a foot in front of me. Quickly I went inside and lit the lamp, but its pale glow dribbled out only a few feet from the door. Beyond was jungle and something else that had no name. It was clear now why Maha Thera had insisted that I make this choice. If I had had any doubt at that moment that it was entirely my decision to come to this forest hut alone, if I had had even the remotest thought that someone else had sent me here, it would have been unbearable.

As the days went by, though, I got used to it. There was always that moment at the fall of darkness when the panic arose, but after a while I just steeled myself against it and stayed inside the hut until it passed. I didn't have to know the particulars of whatever was going on out there. Still there were plenty of surprises.

One day just before lunch I went down to the stream to take my daily bath. This routine was one of the high points of my day. I gathered my bucket, soap, clean clothes, and towel, and gingerly climbed down the steep path that had been carved out of the hill like a tunnel through the underbrush and over-hanging bamboo trees. At the edge of the water I walked off on the felled log that spanned the width of the stream and hopped off in the middle onto a convenient pile of rocks. Standing there I neatly placed my clothes over a tree trunk and prepared to take my bath. All around me were hills, and up river the steamy jungle. There was not a soul in sight, just sounds that by now I had gotten used to: the periodic rustling of branches by monkeys and the buzz of strange insects. Today, though, just as I poured the first bucket over my head I heard an enormous "thump" and then a plop in the water upstream behind me. Turning slowly I saw the form of a huge prehistoric monster. As I stared at the alligatorlike brown scaly body with its long fork-ended tongue whipping the air, my mind grasped for a measure, some standard of distance from my body to the creature's in order to gauge its size. I experienced it as a tiny little inhabitant of the grass, then as an enormous man-eating monster, until my reason settled on some size great enough to call big and frightening. Standing stock still I watched as it stared at me for a long while before making its way up out of the water onto the bank, and then cautiously circling around before dropping into the water again downstream, where it floated away. I was so caught up with my fear and relief that I almost missed the lesson for my living out here alone in the forest.

This environment was a constant confrontation with the unfamiliar. And what my mind didn't recognize, it distorted out of fear. A lizard that might have been six inches long slithering by me became a prehistoric monster. Ominous footsteps in the night were just mice tripping across the rafters. Where was the reality? The automatic nature of fear was becoming more and more apparent to me. Without control over the environment that makes things familiar, fear overwhelms the mind. I had wanted to civilize this place, to set out my little belongings just so, upon my arrival out here, in order to have a recognizable environment when I walked in the door. I was trying to create some format that my consciousness could recognize to keep it from trembling before the unknown. And what would happen if I let go of the format? What would happen if I had let my mind go when it faced that lizard? What would that lizard be? Who would I be?

After I moved out to the *kuti* in the forest, over a week went by without my speaking a word to anyone. Twice a day I would come down the rear of the monastery and wait off in a corner until food was brought to me. Then I would eat silently and alone, not in the dining hall, but in a room separate from the monks. When I finished I would walk without pause up and over the hill back to my seclusion.

As the days of intense practice wore on, a hollow, uncomplicated space developed around me. I wasn't lonely. I didn't crave the contact of other human beings. I became more and more aware of the quiet that comes from the absence of reverbera-tion. Although my mind wasn't silent, without the presence of other minds to reflect, amplify, and distort it, its processes seemed to untangle, to become clear. Most of the tickertape it unwound in the long still hours were messages about my wife. I would be sitting deeply engrossed in some interesting state of concentration when all of a sudden as if the needle had been knocked right across the grooves of the record, a new song with haunting lyrics would be playing through my mind and there I would be, helplessly watching an imagined scene of reunion. The pain that permeated these moments and sometimes stretched into hours is difficult to describe. After a while pain itself be-came the object of my meditation. It was a pain that was in-definable, that's why it hurt so much. Although the longing of my heart seized upon her as its object, it wasn't *her* absence that caused the pain, so real that I could often feel a knot in my chest. I was longing for what I could not find within me. I was plunged into some deep, cold, empty space that is the source of all our desires for other beings, but she was the one who had for so long been the focus of my life. Now absolute solitude made it apparent how much of her I had used to patch that empty space. When I sat absolutely still and silent I could liter-ally feel my body reaching out to try to grasp whatever it thought it needed for completion. *Ego* and *needs* and *neurosis* were explanations that made no sense to me. As I experienced my being on an incredibly direct level, I didn't understand the hole and the pull. I simply felt them. I felt them more than the tangible raw edge of sensuality, more than the urge for tempor-ary union. I felt what preceded that urge. I felt the emptiness itself, and I could almost touch the painful perimeter of my own incompleteness, the unsatisfied hunger for that which I could not experience within myself and had always sought from others. I touched pain itself. Not the situation of pain, nor the object that causes pain. Pain itself. The mechanism that infused my being with moment-to-moment suffering. The empty hole called desire.

It became very clear that the cause of all the pain was desire. I'm sure that I experienced and even fleetingly understood this before, but now it was more than understanding. It was literal experience. Sometimes the clarity and simplicity of this reality brought tears of understanding. Attachment is suffering, that's all there is. Attachment is suffering. And when my mind played out scenes of my wife, then my whole being suffered. Transmuted to shuddering flesh and grimacing minds, it contorted into harsh forms and rigid dimensions. It lumbered like a clumsy animal in an unfamiliar environment, looking warily over its shoulder, stumbling down dark trails. Her, her, her. I felt hands, tongue, and brain reaching greedily, and it was all pure discomfort, pure dis-ease, pure suffering to *be* that way.

There were other times when the attachment eased, when the vision of her and me in some past or future dimension dissolved and all that was left was some gentle reminder of who she really was, some essence of her that looked as lovely at a distance as it did up close, that had no handles on it, that had no use to me, that existed for appreciation, not part of me or even her. I felt then an enormous outpouring of well-wishing, of true good feelings for her happiness. The feelings were not dependent on what she could give me. It was a real letting go of a being who meant so much to me, which is the basis of real love. And in that love there was no suffering.

Sometimes when things were going rather well I would look at myself in the mirror that I carried and laugh. Thinking of my life situation totally amazed me. Most amazing of all was my contentedness with celibacy since most of my adult years had been spent seeking happiness through the company of women. It used to be that a week without sexual contact was difficult to accomplish. Now it had been months and I'd come to understand real celibacy and the false myths of "those terribly frustrated men cooped up behind walls." I understood the difference between denial and real celibacy. There is frustration when there is unsatisfied desire. But real celibacy doesn't describe the absence of sexual activity, rather the absence of the desire for it. Celibacy is a state of mind, not body. After my experiences of the past months it seemed to me a myth that sex is a physical need. My body didn't need it, only because my mind didn't.

During all this time I adhered to a pretty regular schedule, patterned on my stay at the meditation center in Rangoon. By contrast with my schedule, though, there was nothing regular in the routine of my mind. It followed a course that was more like that of a roller coaster. Long, intense spans of high concentration resulting in cool, airy states of mind, which then dissolved into timeless pits of agitation, of bursting at the seams, unable to focus on anything. After four or five days of being out in the hut, this state of agitation had gotten to the point where to make it through the hour until my alarm clock, muffled under a pillow, grumbled that the sitting was over, I was required to clench my jaws in a vicelike manner intertwining my finger tips to keep my arms from flying apart.

Finally one day as soon as I sat down after lunch, I knew that I wasn't going to make it. About half an hour later I threw open the door and marched out into the blazing sun. It was too hot to walk outside. I backed off to the narrow concrete walkway that was shielded by the sloping room overhanging the edge of the hut. I must have paced for a full hour before my mind slowed down enough for me to know what I was doing. Regret set in. I had a feeling of intense frustration that after all I had accomplished in Burma I was back to struggling to sit.

As I continued to walk, I became aware of some intruding presence in my mind which I'd always been aware of but for the first time seemed foreign. Alien. The enormous weight of *should* felt like sacks of rocks across my shoulders. Should what? Should what? Should sit now. I should be sitting for an hour. For what? And then as if I'd just opened my eyes and looked around me at this empty clearing in the forest, I think I noticed for the first time that I was really alone. There was no one here to be even aware of my performance, and yet I was insisting on performing anyway. I was insisting that there was some standard, some way to act, some mode of behavior that would be good if I conformed to it. All my life I was so used to doing it, whatever it was, with my eyes ahead, so used to finishing everything so that it would conform to some expectation while my attention was really over my shoulder hoping to catch a hint of how it was going to be received, that I'd carried all that baggage right down here with me. I hadn't been alone yet. There had always been someone else here. Even when there was no one else here, I was still here.

I stopped my pacing around the hut. The company of this stranger, I, never seemed more clear and more unnatural. There was no reality to him and yet he insisted on staying to watch everything I did. To put a seal of approval or disapproval on it. Where did he even come from? There wasn't enough room in my mind-body for *us*, for this constant war between me doing something and me watching me do it. Why was I afraid to just do it? Because it—I—wouldn't exist? I didn't know. Slowly I began walking again, but I didn't go inside to sit although this was the hour when I "should" sit. I just walked. And now I walked in silence. My steps made no echo. My mind made no leaps to the next step. I felt the incredible freedom from a vise that had always rigidly prescribed each move I made. I had been bound on one side by memory of the past and on the other by worry of the future. Both conditioned my actions in the present moment. Stretched out over that unnatural rack of time I had slowly suffered all these years. But somehow the rack was broken. Each step I took seemed to spring from nothing and dissolve into nothing. Each breath that filled my body as I walked, lived and died faster than I could judge it. On a very simple scale, I understood what freedom was. Nothing pushing and nothing pulling. The clock was dead. Without time nothing could measure me. Nothing could compare me. Each one of my footsteps was uniquely itself. And they led nowhere, only around and around in my empty hut. But somehow although the hut was empty, I was in it. Sitting and yet outside it, walking. That space that was once too small for both of us, now had endless room for none of us. Walking, walking, walking, around the empty hut that was full of me.

I smiled, then giggled, and then wept with laughter. Eyes and ears were not subtle enough senses for the kind of perception that was occurring. For the first time perhaps since I'd been born, I *knew* that I was alive. I knew that I could be . . . and the blank needed no filling in. Finally I opened the door and went back into the hut. Hours went by, interruptions came and went, and I sat and walked and sat and was. The struggle was over. Enormous pain came, enormous agitation came, but they were events and not misunderstandings. The burden of responsibility for creating my life had been lifted from me by the assurance that life creates itself.

9

A Taste of Stillness

Oₙ ᴛʜᴇ ᴍᴏʀɴɪɴɢ ᴏꜰ the tenth day I interrupted my return to the hut following my breakfast to catch my breath on a high flat rock that afforded a view of the entire valley beneath the monastery. The dawn haze had burned off, revealing the neighboring valley, whose sharply edged checkerboard fields stood out in contrast to the surrounding jungle. Perhaps I romanticized by calling this place "jungle" when, in fact, farmland was everywhere. But there is so much unclaimed land in Ceylon that nowhere in the countryside are you so far from the uncultivated forests that you'd not have second thoughts about wandering off in broad daylight, much less in the dark. No cobras here, though, the monks told me. the mongooses made sure of that. One of them was staring at me from a rock higher up the path. His elongated, rodentlike body was covered with prickly fur that made him look as though he'd been dunked in motor oil. His snoutish face was kind of cute, though, and I'd often seen the monks feeding these animals in the courtyard, as a good turn, no doubt, for the animal's appetite for poisonous snakes.

They should have been so kind to the black female dog, Bala, who came scooting out of the forest and leaped up against my legs, yapping wildly until I petted her on the head and pushed her down. The first day I arrived I had casually stroked her. It must have been the first human contact she'd received here aside from kicks and angry words. Since then she went berserk each time she saw me. She would follow me back to my hut and camp outside my door so that I practically tripped over her. A few old monks tried to put a stop to that so she faked it and took a separate trail away from the courtyard to meet me along the way. At first I found her as exasperating as my meditation. But lately I was having such a nice time that she picked up the fringe benefits.

She complained now when I closed the door on her, but I explained that we had no time for our morning circumambulation of the hut, even though the cool shade of the morning was the best time of day for it. I was even eager to start sitting because it was getting so peaceful. I'd been through so many excursions that I'd forgotten that meditation leads to peace of mind.

I sat down and began observing my breath. But my thoughts were still with the pooch. I heard her sniffing outside, feeling sorry for herself I imagined, and I was angry with the monks for the way they treated her. It wasn't very compassionate of them. I tried to figure out why they were so nasty to a dog here. And then remembering my breath, I returned to it. It was so easy to do that I smiled. I had become aware of the fact that I wasn't watching my breath, so I simply began to do it. No recriminations, no jerking away from the thoughts of Bala. No gritting my teeth. I just started again. And again. And again. Because each moment was new. Now was when I was watching the breath. The moment of thinking of the dog was gone, so let it go. Sometimes I would let go of distracting thoughts for so long that my mind took off on long soaring flights of fantasy, dipping and rising like a glider plane. And then I was watching my breath again. And each time I returned to the breath, I was aware of its passage for increasingly longer durations without intervening thoughts. Thoughts would come and I'd let them. The less I did, the stronger the concentration became.

Then I began to observe the sensations in the body. This one, that one, any one. The real event was the shape of my mind. I began to feel the sting of its moment. More and more of them held sensations within my body for objects; fewer and fewer of them reacted to the sensations. The distinction never felt clearer. It was like watching a basketball game on television while an unseen commentator described the action that you could see yourself. The mindless chatter was inessential, yet it continued, and each time you heard it you missed what was going on. But now I was missing less and less. Very quickly I was aware of my entire body as a field of particles, tiny, tiny particles, disappearing, disappearing before I could even say, here they are. Then it seemed as if my mind was spread out through my entire body. Anywhere I focused I felt this single mistlike sensation. And my mind felt as if it was being pulled into this fluid. Should I let go? My attention seemed to gather just below my breastbone, where I often experienced the most violent sensations of all. But that area was quiet now, too. Everything was quiet. For a moment I was confused. It didn't feel like the tingling sensation of dissolution, *anicca*, impermanence. But it grew stronger and I felt pulled toward it.

I was aware of the uniqueness of this sensation, and I wondered how I would describe it. Then as my mind started to phrase the answer, the conceptualizing stopped. The jaws of my chattering mind flapped open in silence. The commentator disappeared.

It only lasted for a moment, perhaps. I can't really be sure, although it was not very long. The next thing I was aware of was an enormous feeling of peace. I started to get up but the sensation within me was so pleasant that I remained for a while longer, enjoying it, until it dissolved back into randomness.

Then I slowly stretched my arms and legs and walked outside. Although I could have sat some more before lunchtime, I didn't feel the need to. Instead I gathered my soap and towel and bucket and started down the far side of the clearing for the river.

It had rained hard the night before and I could hear the water rushing down below as I stood at the top of the steep stairway of rock and log ledges cut into the hillside. Bamboo branches and ferns overhung the stairway so that it seemed like a green tunnel ending at a big fallen tree that spanned the river. I walked out on it about ten feet to the middle, then hopped down onto a pile of large stones on which I could stand and fill my bucket from the swirling waters. I had removed my clothes and was pouring water from the bucket down on my face when I stopped and gazed all around at the winding river, the green hills, the thick jungle. Suddenly I started singing. I couldn't help it, it had been building from the moment I left the hut. Either I would sing or cry; in either case it would not be an expression of sorrow or loneliness but of joy. Standing naked on the rocks, giggling as I doused myself with buckets of cool water, and singing songs of love all the while was not exactly a meditative posture, but there was nothing else I could do.

When I got back to the hut there was still some time before lunch. I certainly couldn't sit, so I began reading some of the books I'd gotten in Burma, but before long I had my notebook out and I was writing. Rather I was planning. I was listing in very precise order my future undertakings. Buddhism, teaching, writing, studying, living. My life seemed perfectly clear to me. What would I do, where would I live, how would I get on? All of that seemed beside the point. I felt that I had an understanding of a process that transcended events or situations. I punctuated that last inspiration with an exclamation point and headed off for lunch followed by my love-starved dog, Bala.

It was a great lunch. They all were. Ceylon might be scrounging for food but the monks in this forest monastery would be the last to know about it. I couldn't believe that they expected anyone to be able to move, much less meditate, after finishing the enormous quantities of rice, curries, chutneys, potatoes, fruits, and sweets they piled on the table. But today, I suppose, I was willing to try. A monk in training watched with glee as I worked my way through the entire mountain of lovely, semipolished rice that I usually nibbled from. When I had finished my last papaya slice with a burp, he looked at me and motioned with the flat of his hand at his mouth, imitating my gesture to show they'd given me too much. "Full?" he asked, not quite sure it was the word I used.

"You bet," I answered, reluctantly getting up. Instead of returning to my hut right away I walked back to the meditation quarters and had tea with Sunno and another friend.

It was midafternoon when I got back to my place and since there was nothing else to do, I started meditating. The difficulties of the first hour I put down to just getting settled after my first contact with people in nearly a week, but the second hour wasn't much better. My mind felt like a pressure cooker. Ideas, plans, inspirations were building in it and every time I tried to apply a little direction, by focusing on my breath, the pot threatened to explode. I got up and walked around the hut. When I sat again it was still no better. During the next two days I must have walked a hundred miles around that hut. I sat for eight hours each day, but nothing whatsoever was happening, except an endless spiral of joyous inspiration. And then I'd get up again and walk around and sing old songs and try to remain vaguely mindful of what I was doing. Finally this pattern just became too exhausting, and I suppose I was getting a little guilty. It was time to somehow put a stop to it. Despite an instant inner resistance to reining in my wandering mind I forced myself to sit longer.

The effect was very strange. The concreteness of my mind's activities began to disintegrate. There were no recognizable thoughts, but I still couldn't concentrate. A vague sort of cloud surrounded my mind and it engulfed me for indefinite lapses of time before I could shake myself free and begin watching my breath again. As the day wore on this cloud became thicker and deeper, and I had a harder time pulling myself out of it. When I did, I was left with a strange, shivering feeling in my body as if I was touching dead flesh.

Suddenly I was frightened by how far I'd strayed from meditation in the past two days. I set the alarm clock for two hours later and hid it under my pillow to muffle its ticking. Then I began to sit. It wasn't easy. I could only stay in place by gritting my teeth and concentrating on the clenched muscles of my jaw. But I continued sitting because despite my inability to focus on anything at all, I felt some enormous inner pressure building. It wasn't a physical pain. It felt more as if every cell was suffering from a migraine headache. I sank into it, and it became darker and duller. My mind's dialogue was reduced to nonsense words, then indistinct, slurred syllables, then a steady, low, deathly moan. Thunder rumbled. At first it seemed to come from within me, but when I heard shrieking monkeys and the shattering of branches as they scrambled for cover, I knew it was definitely outside.

As the thunder grew louder the air chilled and a cold, damp wave crept through my body, penetrating deeper and deeper from the skin inward until I was shivering. The lamp in the room faded. From the booming thunder I could tell the storm was nearly overhead. Then it arrived, and the clay tile roof rattled under the force of the rain. When I opened my eyes, the room was in complete darkness. When I closed my eyes again, the darkness increased, beyond blackness. For a moment I tried to explain it. Then I stopped and watched numbly as whatever light remained in my mind faded to a kind of cold void, completely empty of forms or shapes. The rain continued to roar against the roof. I was sure it was pouring into the hut, and that I should get up and try to plug the leaks or just mop up the water. But I continued to sit. Something in me was both fascinated and too terrified by the events for me to move. I didn't want to open my eyes. When I finally recognized what it was that kept me rooted in my place I nearly screamed. The room felt full; I could feel the stultifying presence of beings everywhere around me, as close as the rafters above my head. I sat there in the rain and thunder while my nerves were blasted for as long as I could. It seemed that the storm would not end until I ended it. There was an uttterly strange sensation in my body, one that I did not recognize. My eyes cracked open and I saw toothy, grotesque faces that stared at me from crowds miles deep. My heart almost stopped. Somehow, though I wasn't even aware of it, I got up and lit the lamp.

Finally I found myself standing in the open doorway, watching the remains of the storm disperse over the forest, leaving the sky purple and bruised. I was so sure that I was not insane, that if I was, then I was so insane that it would never matter. Furthermore, nothing that had happened had in the least contradicted what I had been told by a line of teachers right back to the Buddha. I had always ignored the notion of planes of existence as they are called, or relegated it to the level of mythological window dressing. Beings are reborn into forms which we can see, human and animal, and into forms we ordinarily can't see. We call them demons or angels. Where? Down in the center of the earth where the hellfires burn? I turned slowly and examined the inside of my hut.

The fact that it *looked* empty now was of no comfort. I knew what was there. I fell on my bed and was asleep in minutes. But numerous times during the night I woke up suffocating from dreams of flesh-devouring demons. I had to sit up and focus all my attention on my chest to find my breath again. Finally, before dawn, I gave up on any chance of sleep and just made myself comfortable sitting on my pillow. It seemed that I might as well look at the demons awake as asleep.

In an instant, though, they were gone. My body felt clean and clear, my mind light. I'd forgotten what such a feeling was like. It was parachuting back to earth, to that space of peace I'd come to three days before. Everything hung together motionless as it had then. Quickly, in a moment of balance, my mind saw where it had been and what had occurred. In a brief instant of understanding all was explained. I got up and sat down at my desk and opened my notebook. After recording the hour, the date, and the number of days since my arrival at the monastery I began.

I have experienced the moment of *nirvana*. Not today, not this hour. Three mornings ago. Only I did not recognize it then. That was its nature. Nothing of the past, no memory, association, wish, or desire entered that moment. "The conceptualizing stopped." That was my only description for it. It had taken this long for my mind to grasp that experience conceptually. Why I had trouble recognizing it then, and why it appeared clear to me only now, was, I thought, part of the nature of the experience. As long as you can think about it and say, "it is like this or like this," then you are still within this mundane realm. I could only record the events that preceded it, and then, "the conceptualizing stopped." But now, for reasons I don't understand, I am drawn back to that moment. I see once again the stuttering of my mind as it tries to react before the experience totally overwhelms it into silence.

I wonder what it was all about. What is this *nirvana?* Clearly I am not the Buddha. That, I think, is what is known as final *nirvana*, where the birth and death process, purified of all desires, ends, and there is no further rebirth. But there is also the state of *nirvana* that one experiences in this lifetime. It is taught that there are four stages of "holiness" that begin with the first instant, the mind's first moment of *nirvana*. In Burma they talk about the "taste" of *nirvana*. I'm not sure whether this is the same as that first stage of holiness or not, because that first stage means that one has attained a place in the Stream and that it is only a matter of seven lifetimes or less before that person achieves final *nirvana*. Why? Because to experience even one moment of *nirvana*, all belief in the existence of an ego, an I, must be gone.

Have I done this? I don't know. I believe that I had an experience of *nirvana*, but I don't feel that I have arrived at any state. I think I experienced the moment of egolessness, when there was nobody to conceptualize the experience, when the moment was all. But what about now? Who is writing this? I am aware of myself, though I don't believe in that self's reality. So I'm probably who I was a week ago, maybe, or perhaps I'll stop worrying, content that for that moment when I wasn't there, *nirvana* was.

10

The Great Elder

AFTER TWO WEEKS OF isolation in the forest, I left the monastery for a short time, mostly to find out about the possibility of returning to Burma. It had been rumored that tourist visas to that country were going to be extended longer than seven days. If so, I could return there soon, and possibly stay for as long as a month. The rumors proved false, however, and I was left with a very open end to my trip. There was no particular rush to get back to Burma now, since that would probably be the last stop on my way home. And I certainly wasn't ready to return home.

As I was about to leave the monastery the American anthropologist named Michael, who'd been doing periodic fieldwork here for a year, arrived. We'd met briefly in Colombo and it was from him that I had first learned about this forest monastery. We took an instant liking to each other and he ended up driving me back to Colombo and putting me up at his home while I searched for a visa. After a few days in the city, though,

I couldn't wait to return to the monastery. Michael noticed my haste and urged me to relax and take a trip to the interior, to Kandy, the cultural capital of Ceylon, where I might meet some of the eminent Ceylonese and Western Buddhists who often gathered there. Among the Western monks, he said, was an old German named Nyanaponika, who had come to Ceylon some forty years ago and was one of a small group of European Buddhists long resident in Ceylon. They had founded a place called the Island Hermitage, down the coast from Colombo, a monastery devoted not only to the practice of meditation but also to rendering into English important works of Theravada Buddhism, the branch known in the West as Hinayana, and the prevalent form of Buddhism in southeast Asia and Ceylon.

"It must have been quite a time back then," Michael mused as we sat on the porch of his colonial-style home in a comfortable suburb of Columbo. "The romance of it all. Expatriates in yellow robes. The British raj and exotic teachings." He put down his cold drink and described the Island Hermitage, which still functions today and is accessible only by small boat. He conjured up images of the Quest, the religious journey to be free of all past conditioning, all patterns, all ties. But in recent years, Nyanaponika had retired to a more solitary situation, a place called the Forest Hermitage, located in Kandy, which was in the interior of Ceylon.

"You should go up to Kandy, you know, and see Nyanaponika. He's one of the last who's left and he's getting on in years. You can get a glimpse of what it was like."

So I set out for Kandy looking for the past and perhaps some clue to my future. On the train ride up I read a book by Nyanaponika which Michael gave me, *The Heart of Buddhist Meditation*. It enthralled me, the way a powerful novel used to. It was the first coherent description I had found in writing of what I'd been doing for months now.

Kandy was a gorgeous city. The cultural heart of Ceylon lay on lush hills overlooking a large, tree-lined lake. The trees were very special. Giant parasols whose span equaled their height, they leaned out uniformly from the banks far over the water. In April at the onset of the hot season, Kandy's cool, gardenlike atmosphere was a welcome contrast to the city streets of Columbo.

On arriving in Kandy, I went directly to the small house at the far end of the lake that was the headquarters of the Buddhist Publication Society and of the *Wheel*, a small quarterly that published the writings of Nyanaponika and others. I told the gentleman in charge, Richard Abeyasekere, an elderly, white haired Ceylonese layman of elflike appearance, about my activities over the past few months and asked him how I might meet Nyanaponika. Richard offered to escort me the next day, to the Forest Hermitage, where Nyanaponika lived. Meanwhile, he invited me to be his house guest.

The next morning, just after breakfast, we set off walking through Kandy past the enormous white Temple of the Tooth, a sacred shrine that supposedly houses an actual relic of the Buddha's body. Then we turned away from the lake along a path that led into a steep climb through the surrounding forest. The path we chose was lined with enormous mahogany trees covered with thick vines of spade-shaped, dark green leaves. The trees housed thousands of bats whose shrieks filled the forest. Richard had remarkable vigor for a man his age and trying to keep up with him reminded me how out of shape I'd gotten sitting on my butt all these months. As I puffed up the hill I tried to formulate the exact wording of the questions I hoped to ask Nyanaponika. Both Michael and Richard had made it clear that the old monk already had too many Westerners stopping by these days merely for social calls. He would be quite happy, though, to discuss any questions I might have about technical matters.

We arrived at a neat set of small cottagelike buildings at a clearing at the top of a hill. Nyanaponika himself answered the door. He was a large, cheerful-looking man of powerful, vigorous appearance and indeterminate age. His large, bony hands looked old but strong. His face was like a baby's, though, pink with ears that jutted out, and he had an almost childlike smile and twinkling eyes of wonder. Richard briefly introduced me and I explained my purpose, as well as what I considered my credentials in the meditation profession. This seemed to be an acceptable calling card, and we were invited in. After he and Richard had discussed some business about the next issue of the *Wheel*, Nyanaponika, adjusting his long yellow robes over his shoulder, seated himself behind his desk and offered me a chair. Then after a few brief pleasantries, he asked me just what I had in mind. Luckily I had it all written down. For the next half hour I phrased the questions as best I could and Nyanaponika gave clear and detailed replies. He spoke wonderful English with a German inflection, and his long, rolling sentences were punctuated at regular intervals by *"Nein?"* which was not a nervous pause, or even a question, but almost a metrical device to focus my attention on important points. But as he answered and I carefully took notes, it became clear to me that I wasn't here for information, at least not this kind of information.

I was here for something else. Let me know about you, Maha Thera, Great Elder. Let me know about *how* you are. This life you lead, this wonderful existence in quiet solitude at the top of a forested hill overlooking a lake in a beautiful tropical town. Working alone, apart from the daily drivel that I can't approach anymore. Tell me what it's like to leave your home for forty years? That's really what I wanted to know. But instead of asking that I filled pages of my note book with his replies and asked more questions, getting involved in the asking because something more than the words was passing between us. I felt the tempo of our interchange pick up, Nyanaponika's wide, open mind come to bear against my own, forcing it to dig deeper, to penetrate. His energy was astounding. Rigorous, German, I might have said, but as I looked at him, I didn't see a German or a European, or a Ceylonese or even a Buddhist monk. He was Man, free, one who had laid down all trappings, all the baggage everyone carries around to set up shop wherever he or she goes. He looked like one whose past was truly erased. Focusing on him was difficult. I looked at his face and kept seeing a baby with eyebrows bobbing excitedly as he spoke. His swaddling robes often slipped off his shoulder. What are you doing here in Ceylon? I felt like shouting, but I had the eerie feeling he would have shrugged and perhaps replied, "I don't know, but it's a nice place, *nein?*"

My questioning, our conversation, was becoming personal. We weren't talking about abstractions, but about meditation and about experience. Nyanaponika explained in detail a kind of psychology that he'd outlined in his book, the process of mindfulness, the observation of the entire mind-body in its various parts. Finally, our discussion ended and we both sat there smiling happily.

After a short pause we began talking again, this time about books. He took me over to his shelves, which held an enormous range of literature, philosophy, and religion. Science fiction, humanistic psychology, and Buddhist texts sat side by side. He kept showing me facets, new sides, new avenues of knowledge he'd explored, new means of expression. He wasn't only a scholar but a poet as well, as his marvelous translations of Buddhist texts showed.

When he finally saw me to the door, he asked me how long I'd be in Kandy and whether I might want to return to visit him. Outside the doorway other visitors were waiting, a professor of Indian studies from Yale and his wife. They had been waiting out there for some time. Nyanaponika apologized to them for the delay and smiled at me again. I told him I'd surely be back, and asked if the day after next would be too soon. He smiled and seemed almost as glad as I.

Richard seemed to work at his job three hundred and sixty-five days a year and I don't know how many hours a day. He was usually still at his desk when I went to sleep. I helped him a little, proofreading galleys, but much of my time I kept wandering around his library, opening books that led me to other books that led me back to my notebook to jot down questions for my next meeting with Nyanaponika. At other times I went by myself for long walks into town for dinner, which Richard did without, or just around the lake. I spent a lot of time beside the lake, trying to piece together the fragments of recent experiences, feeling them all pointing in a single direction. Richard was fond of telling me stories of Nyanaponika's younger days when he was just one of a group of disciples gathered around Nyanatiloka, the German monk who founded the Island Hermitage. The stories encompassed all the details of romantic adventure: exotic locales, powerful personages, and even tragic lives. But the real adventure, at least to me, was the abandonment of everything familiar in one's life to take up the single task of seeking enlightenment.

Richard's stories only rekindled within me a growing fascination for this ultimate adventure. During the last few days before I left the monastery, I had spent some time with the two English-speaking monks, Sunno and Ratanapala, at their quarters, the meditation section of the complex, where a small number of *bhikkus* lived in seclusion to pursue more intensive practice. I had gotten quite close to both of them over numerous cups of afternoon tea. Now one brief incident stuck in my mind. Ratanapala was an intense, dark man of about forty with jet black eyes and a constant bristly stubble of beard, who had only been a monk some three years after managing his father's exporting business in Columbo. When we talked of his life he said it had only one purpose, to achieve some sort of freedom, some taste of freedom in this lifetime. Nothing outside these walls was of any interest to him anymore. "For three years," he said, "I've been in this place and never gone outside it. And I won't," he added, "until I die."

As I listened to Richard now I was only reminded of the seemingly unbridgeable gap between what these men as monks had left behind and the life they were pursuing now. And here I was trying to keep one foot on both sides of the chasm. It was getting uncomfortable. My discomfort had become apparent to me immediately on leaving the monastery with Michael, when we stopped for a day and a night at a beautiful house on the beach rented by two friends of his, a Western couple. It was a very worldly household, complete with balky servants, lovely food, sick pet animals, fine swimming, car repairs, good beer, and marital squabbles. It was all perfectly familiar to me while at the same time disturbingly alien. I understood what Ratanapala meant. All my life the mundane details of daily existence on the planet had always been an imposition, an unwanted intrusion on . . . something else . . . something more important. Even when I'd never been able to identify what really was more important. Now, it seemed, I had. It couldn't be clearer. And more importantly, here was an actual working model, a way of life which men were living, where those details and consuming diversions didn't exist. Renunciation. Something that isn't undertaken lightly.

At some moments it seemed totally unthinkable, just too distant from who I was and what I wanted and what I would have to leave behind. And in other moments I was already there. I was the monk Ratanapala, happy to give the past up forever. But could I do it? Only I would know, surely, but somehow I looked to these men, particularly Nyanaponika, for some clue.

In preparation for my next meeting with Nyanaponika I had begun reading some pretty interesting books on the Theravada tradition, the school of Buddhism which traces its lineage back to the original sermons of the Buddha. Along the way it has developed perhaps the most detailed maps of spiritual development ever conceived, describing a topography of the mind that is at first incomprehensible to a Westerner. Enormous manuals of psychology dissect such phenomena as moments of consciousness, stages of mental purification, components of various mind states, and every single step from here to enlightenment.

Wading through these texts I was startled to find very detailed descriptions of mind states that corresponded to my actual experiences. I was eager to pinpoint where I was on this map, but the basic compass points were not entirely clear to me. *Nirvana* was the goal, I assumed. But the texts talked of it as if it was two different things, a final, absolute release from suffering and rebirth, and a momentary experience, a contact with that wholly other state right here in this life. Was that what I had experienced that day in my hut, that instant of stillness that had so blasted me apart for days after? Was that moment *nirvana?* And if it was, where was it on this map of enlightenment?

It was evening and I was sitting in Richard's office poring over more books when the old monk came in unexpectedly. He had walked all the way down the hill to discuss the cover for a forthcoming issue of the *Wheel.* I smiled politely when he entered and tried to continue reading. When he was about to leave, he asked if I would like to accompany him at least part of the way on his walk back. I quickly followed him, but I was nervous because I hadn't fully formulated my questions. I tried to explain them as we walked, but he didn't seem to be listening. He was too busy pointing out the sights and landmarks. We took a detour to the back of the Temple of the Tooth, where he showed me a very ancient building and explained its history and style of architecture. What about *nirvana?* I wanted to blurt out, but he seemed perfectly satisfied that our walk should be taken up with matter-of-fact conversation. He took a joyous interest in everything that passed before him.

I asked him to tell me a little about his own life, and he talked of how he had come to read some books in Germany and then decided to come here. Not why or how, just that he ended up here. Then he spoke glowingly about the old days at the Island Hermitage, the days when there were quite a few monks, all embarking on their unique path. I asked if he went back there anymore.

"No," he said. "It is finished now for me. I spend most of my time up here. There are still plenty of monks there now, but no strong personalities there anymore." He seemed to say that at least for him the grand adventure was over. "There aren't many foreign monks in Ceylon anymore," he commented without saying why. I had a real sense of having come in on the tail end, the last chapter of a great story. But I knew that he would never say that. For him it was just another day now, things just happened to be different. He went on with his work and was not concerned about his age or the future, while I, it seemed, had an entire lifetime ahead of me to worry about. What would I do with it? What *should* I do with it, I wanted to ask, but didn't know how. Can I really live like you? Or Bhikku Sunno and Bhikku Ratanapala? That was the question that I really needed an answer to.

We were getting pretty far up the hill. The sun was almost setting and I'd have to turn back soon. I hadn't yet asked what I really wanted to. Finally I said, "Would you mind very much if I ask you some questions about my own meditation? You see it's been a while since I've been with a teacher and a lot of things have been happening, and maybe you could help me to understand them."

"All right," he said rather carefully, "if it's possible." Then I went on to describe my meditation practice and that one particular event in the forest hut. It was confusing, I said, because I was having trouble correlating my own experience with the technical descriptions I had read. Tell me, I was trying to say, what I have experienced.

He responded by saying that one had to be careful of what one read and heard. The most important thing in this meditation practice was always to remain critical, absolutely critical of whatever you experienced. Whatever the state of consciousness I experienced was, I should at least take it as an encouraging sign, as a hint of what lay beyond, and continue on.

I thought about this for a moment in silence. Nyanaponika very matter-of-factly remarked that it was time for me to turn back or it would be too dark to find my way down the hill. It was only as I walked alone through the forest dusk that I realized how understated the old monk had made his good-bye. The noncommittal nature of his answer to my question didn't really upset me. I knew as I walked back down the hills alone, that I wanted all kinds of advice and judgment from him. I wanted to hear, "This is the life, the way, the path; follow it."

But none of it was that clear ever. I'd be lucky to make it down the hill before dark.

I'd come here for a day or two, reluctantly. When Richard woke me early the next morning in time to make the first train back to Colombo, I had no real idea why I was leaving so soon. It had been my plan, of course, and I wanted to return to the intensive practice in the monastery. But at the same time I could have stayed in Kandy, earning my keep perhaps by helping Richard with his publications. When I went into the kitchen with my bags packed, Richard had breakfast prepared for me. I felt as if I was leaving a dear friend I'd known for a lifetime. I felt my whole life accelerating, without my will or control. I felt more confident than ever of its direction, but all the time there was less and less to hold onto, less and less to be sure of.

11

The Path of Power

THE LIGHT OF GOD. Ishvara, the Lord. Divine Luminescence. Seen with the mind's eye only through a mind that can see. I stared with eyelids drawn immobile at an empty black background. The shimmering disk of cool brilliance was not an object but an event, which eyes cannot see. My attention stayed with my breath as it had for days, the tiny touch of my life against thin skin. The awareness on that single point was almost unbroken. That stillness of mind created the light, the light that cannot be seen, only known, until I felt the light, breathed light as a tingly, glowing star.

In the space that had no measurements, between me and the light, the pull toward union grew. The light was a doorway in space to some other dimension. The Gateway to God. Can I go to him? Will he come to me? There can be no time. My being was at ease in the glowing proximity of its own light. The mind had come down to just that. Its beginningless formations, endless ruminations, vast wells of hatreds and desires had all been momentarily subdued, replaced by an empty beam that shone into the darkness of my mind, producing clear, white light.

I was aware of it across a chasm of silent space, at the bottom of which lay my stilled mind, whose movement had been shackled by the continuous awareness of the breath moving in, moving out, moving in, moving out. When the mind is still, its nature is light. I perched warily on the edge of the chasm, conscious of the sleeping monster below, aware of the pull to the luminescence across the expanse of nothing. I'd stepped out toward it before, seeking to become one with that light as it beckoned me, and the movement plunged me down into the awakened darkness of my mind come quickly alive.

Now I sat stock still. Nothing else could be done. To put attention on the light is to snuff it out, *because it is not there.* It is not available to any of the mind's senses or to thought. Only when thought and senses are absolutely stilled by the continuous awareness of that single point of breath is the light manifest. And as the light became clearer, sharper, and brighter, it beckoned across that chasm of space.

My only lure was patience, calmly observing without reaction the shower of bright comets and flashing meteors across the dark sky of my mind. Returning to my breath, until the flashings of light coalesced into a single disk that pulsed with each breath. I felt anticipation rising and immediately let that feeling go. The need to let go of the rising thoughts was continuous as the intensity of the light grew and beckoned, *Come to me.* I quickly let go of the thought, lest the mind monster at the bottom of the chasm take shape in that thought.

The tempo quickened until my mind, as if buoyed upon a cresting wave, rode above the thoughts, straight ahead to dead silence. And the light was sharper, clearer, closer than I'd ever known it. I stood to balance on the wave, relaxed, sure that I was at my goal, when without warning the light flared into a brilliance that blinded me, threw me off balance, plunged me under into blackness. Falling, falling, all I heard were shrieks of laughter.

Slowly I stretched my legs out and got up. It was only mid-afternoon. A certain numbness pervaded my consciousness. It had been this way for nearly a week now. I noticed that I was standing immobile in the room, not yet back in my body. I opened the shutters on the windows. The brilliant heat of midday was already fading. I felt as though I was coming down off some powerful drug. A hallucinogen? No, it was all too real. How long? About a week since I returned to the monastery from my brief sojourn with Nyanaponika at Kandy. And since then? Light years. My own pun amused me. Light, light. The prize of mystics through the ages. The illumination of God, but to these sober Buddhists it is only *nimitta*, the sign, sign of the mind's concentration. No God. No nothing, Just the mind, and that is but a hollow process.

From the beginning I'd been taught that there is concentration and insight. The first is the tool, the other the way. Until recently the sharpening of the tool, the repetitious observation of the breath, the development of the ability to hold the attention on one single point, had been gruesome work. Until, almost unexpectedly, I found my attention gently anchored to the passage of the breath, unperturbed by the events within and without it. Its expansions, contractions, ripples, or wheezes didn't alter the attention. Nor did the screams of birds or other forest sounds. I was amazed. As if a switch had been thrown, my consciousness leaped into a different mode, and the connection between my awareness and the event of my breath became so profound that all the other events of mind—its fears, desires, burbling disquiet, painful aches, and droopy torpor—simply vanished. In one instant! Not slowly, gradually rubbed out, but gone.

I stretched my arms up over my head, pretending to act normally. I couldn't really remember that state of mind. The mind-cooling periods of stillness on the pillow were followed by hot explosions of irrational fear, loud thumps of leaves against the roof, and the dreadful marching of mice on the rafters. I was hacking my way through a jungle. The process had been simplified to stillness only, yet I was at every instant struggling with the desire of my being *not* to be still. I was more and more becoming a boulder in the stream. And as the water rushed by, more ferociously in the narrowing path, beginningless, endless water of time and mind, I felt its force wearing at me. If I relented for a moment, I was swept along with it, plunged back into the torment of random thought, and the hell of my unbridled mind. I couldn't tell whether the periods of stillness made the chaos more intense just by comparison, or whether my stilled, increasingly powerful mind states were diving deeper and deeper into chaos.

I stood in the doorway of my hut staring emptily ahead, considering, as much as my mind was capable of such thought process, where this was all taking me. I could feel that I was at a crossroads. In one direction was the uniquely Buddhist practice of Insight, in which the mind observes whatever passes before it and lets go. It learns emptiness, it becomes empty. It holds to no state, no bliss, no high. It simply is. But the other path the Buddha knew well, too, the path of *Jhana*. It is the traditional path to mystic states. To God, if you think he's there, or, if like the Buddha you know that nothing is there, then still you recognize that states of mind exist, powerful trance states where the ordinary mind process is interrupted, replaced by experiences of bliss and supreme joy.

Teachers in Burma had told me that these states of *Jhana*, as they are called, are dangerous. They are the road to power, not wisdom. Through them one develops supernormal powers, like reading minds, telekinesis, or being in two places at once, all very clearly outlined in the ancient manuals of Buddhist psychology.

The powers didn't particularly attract me. And I'm not sure I believed in their availability. The states of mind, though, were clearly an attraction. It was, to me, power of a different sort. Not power to do anything. Power just to be. I felt it in the enormous calm, and even in the trembling fears. I could negotiate the fears; I'd learned to relax when they seemed over-whelming—as they did right now as I stared blankly out my doorway—and to proceed again when they had passed.

Intuitively now I read the signals of my mind-body. A psychic overload warning flashed. Idling in a doorway was not enough. The pressure that the late hours on the pillow had built was threatening to explode. I had to open valves. I sat down in the chair at the table and slowly poured myself a cup of tea from the thermos and stirred in a few heaping teaspoonfuls of raw sugar. My notebook was my raft when the waters got too treacherous for swimming. I took it out, marked "day 7" and the date at the top of a clean page, sipped some more of my beverage, and began writing.

The gentle diversion of searching for words and the atten-tion-consuming activity of actually moving the pen were ground wires in the storm. I described my dips and peaks of mind, smiling at them from a distance. The going was heavy, but I decided I was managing through it.

As I dotted the end of the last sentence, an explosion of thunder punctuated it, and the roof rattled under an assault of rain. Standing at the open door I saw large puddles all around the hut already, and long founts of water streaming from the corners of the roof. I suddenly remembered that this morning I had thought about paying a teatime visit to Sunno in his quar-ters as he had invited me to. The thick curtain of rain now put an end to any such notion. It would have been nice to have tak-en a walk just now, to get out of the hut for a while, to speak some words. I'd heard no sound except my own voice for a week. I thought about saying something aloud if only to myself. No, I shouldn't. I turned quickly back into the room. What to do? I'd already written in my notebook and had my tea for the day. I approached the bed. It seemed out of the question to med-itate more right now. My mind was accelerating. I walked to the desk, numbly opened the notebook and stared at the last page of what I had just written. It seemed like a weak joke. "Heavy going, but managing well." I grimaced. Only an hour ago.

Writing is such a lie, perpetrating the illusion that the past can be retained. I dropped the book and thought the table would collapse under its weight. The room was assuming rude proportions. The acceleration continued. I made no effort to stop it. I was paralyzed, with no words of self-encouragement. I could whistle no happy tunes.

I found myself sitting on the front step, a downpour just inches from my face, my mind rummaging through possibilities of escape from the state that could only be described as insanity. Complete dissociation. Images and thought at random. Then like a boulder smashing against my head, there was the realization that in the next instant I could be stark, raving mad. My only choice was to stumble up that raving hill through a forest of terrors to seek safety with a yellow-robed gang who didn't speak English anyway.

I heard the soundless scream of chaos. Then silence. I was aware of my breath. I felt its touch and responding automatically, I got up and closed the doors and shutters. When I sat on the bed I felt my eyes drop behind their own curtains. I was alone. Suddenly the thoughts were whispers and I was aware of mindlight. Sharp, distinct. A tiny glowing disk. By keeping my attention firmly rooted to the breath, I could expand the light to a burning saucer, shrink it to a tiny pinpoint of brightness, and then blow it up to light the entire universe. Then slowly the light contracted and stabilized as a tiny sphere of perception. I watched in awe, and then unmistakably felt a beckoning, an actual pull toward the light, as if it were holding out a hand, bidding me to come. I didn't have to decide, I was sucked forward. I tumbled toward it, into it, through it, vitally aware all the while. Perceptions flowed through new channels, and my entire being welled up with joy. I'd been transported, rematerialized in a different universe. Time was glutted. Mindbody was soaked in bliss.

Guided by that storm I was soaring as if my body had been pumped full of joy by the bellows of bliss. It could go on forever, it could go on forever, this was the tacit understanding. I wasn't holding on to anything. I was there. I was in this other place. Perhaps I'd never return, perhaps there was no way out. Thought faded; experience overwhelmed it. An enormous joy, a consuming exuberance overtook me. Took me away.

Finally I brought it to an end. Perhaps I was too dizzy to continue. My clock indicated that two and a half hours had gone by. Slowly I untangled my body, which had been returned to me. It was dark outside. I stood in the open doorway waiting for the fact of time's passage to register properly. To mean something. I looked around the room. Its strangeness was unmistakable. Not like before, before, when, I recall, I was insane. And what was I now? Thought had not yet returned to normal. I still felt that other realm where thought was rendered superfluous.

What to do? There was not much to occupy the time in a hut like this. My hands lit the kerosene lamp and searched out the notebook. I began to write, but the words felt cumbersome, unwieldy. Sentences hung together like chicken wire. Why was I writing anyway? What made what had just happened so important that I was throwing out nets to capture it? Why couldn't I let go of it?

In a fit of inspiration I blew out the lamp and tiptoed back to bed, carefully smoothed out the cushions, and sat. Why write when I could be there? An hour went by, and I was still unable to disengage myself from the randomness of my mind. Unable to fly. I probed and searched for the keyhole in the invisible door that opened onto the other dimension. I feigned stillness. But no one was fooled.

Finally I got up again, lit the lamp, and poured the last cup of tea from the still warm thermos. It was getting late in the evening but I wasn't close to being sleepy. I found myself pacing the floor until I realized that I was hanging out, waiting for the next round. Time on my hands. Looking for something to do! Like a junkie waiting for a connection. The dark hints of danger along this strange path of *Jhana* that my teachers in Burma had given me suddenly were apparent. Not the powers that could be developed. They were leagues away. No right here in the first plunge was the real danger. *It felt good! And I wanted more!*

Screeeeeeeeeetch! Chug-a-chug-a, chug-a-chug-a, chug-a-chug-a. (Jump of my mind. Time in reverse.) A first-class train compartment speeding toward Benares. Travis stretched out on the lower berth across from me. The remains of our sumptuous fruit and nut salad on the floor. Memories of Goenka and the Jain temple glowing like the setting sun behind us. Heading for a new day. "This, my boy, is the good life." Cool evening breezes from wide-open fields brush our faces comfortably. The talk turns to good old days. We are reminded of our trips and adventures. Fine beaches. Fine mornings, with fine women in cafes after wine all night. Exotic tales of Sumatra and Malaysia. Hotels we both knew.

"I'm ready," Travis smiled nostalgically. "We can blow off the meditation course and be in Goa by late afternoon tomorrow."

"And then?" I asked.

"We'd be bored by the weekend," he sighed. Travis swung his legs down to the floor. "I think this meditation is a bit of a trap."

"How so?"

"Well, why did you start it, anyway? To get high, right? That's really it, isn't it? I mean, one day after you'd been grubbing through your life for twenty years someone gave you something to swallow and it blew your brains out. Everything you used to worry about didn't matter at all, but twelve hours later it was over. So that's when you set out for the beaches, right. And the moving and the traveling and never staying anywhere long enough to know last names. And that was really high. Until the edge wore off or the dope made you psychotic. And then? Someone tells you about the ultimate high. The experience with no end. Meditation. Just sit still and be quiet."

I waited. "And now?"

Travis shrugged, "You know what's now. Are you high?

Am I high? I'm right here. Being equanimous. Seeing all things the same so nothing can get us high. And we feel guilty if it does. It's all the same. Beaches and train stations. What's the difference? Only our minds make the difference. There's nothing to get excited about. I can't believe anymore in the things that used to get me high. And that's tough, 'cause there's still part of me that wants that *hit*, that bliss, that flying-over-the-rainbow rush. I don't want to know that what I'm flying on won't last, that it all fades and I'll crash if I don't let go. But part of me does know it. So I have a hard time getting off the ground. But I keep trying. Half the truth is painful."

The compartment was nearly dark. Travis's words had spiced the cool air with sadness.

The hut was cool and dark. I stepped outside under a starful sky. It was calming, a step away from chaos, terror, and bliss. I felt I had learned something. I had a sense of where I was heading, and it was not in the right direction. Not the path I had started out upon. With each step, I was getting farther and farther from insight. I had ceased witnessing the process and had become, once again, an eager participant, flying and crashing and suffering. I had given up understanding for enjoying. And enjoyment never lasts.

This soaring flight of *Jhana* had been a wonderful teacher. It had been much easier, by comparison, to develop equanimity toward pain and to understand its emptiness and its impermanence, because I *wanted* to work through pain, to go beyond it. Bliss is much harder to let go of, but in the holding on there is nothing but suffering. The holding is the pain. This moment, now, under a sky full of stars and a cool tropical breeze with a forest breathing bedtime symphonies, this was it. Not memories of other mind states or yearning for their return. Buddha was right. God may make you happy, but even he can't end your suffering. Only knowing will.

12

The Great Blind Sea Turtle

On my return to the monastery from my brief journey out into the world, I had been warmly greeted by the head monk, Nyayaka Maha Thera, and by my two friends *Bhikkus* Sunno and Ratanapala, who were convinced that I had returned for good. It was quite a homecoming. I asked Sunno if he might like to take a walk out to my hut one afternoon and have some tea so we could talk. He was quite pleased by the invitation and promised to visit me soon. The days went by, though, and he didn't come. One day after lunch, I sent the young boy who served me food back into the meditation quarters to fetch Sunno. I didn't think it proper for me simply to wander in there unexpectedly. Sunno appeared with a big smile, and after apologizing for not being able to make it to my *kuti*, invited me to his quarters.

I was glad to enter the serenity of the meditation quarters. In the middle of the courtyard there was a large, glass-enclosed Buddha shrine. We entered through delicate mahogany doors, and I felt intoxicated by the fragrance of floral offerings, elaborately arranged on brass trays at the feet of the statue. It was a nice reminder of the peacefulness of the monastery. Lately I'd found it somewhat distracting when I came down for my twice-daily meals to find many of the monks standing around in little groups, talking and laughing about nothing in particular, and certainly, it seemed, not about the holy life.

I knew that the monks who seriously practiced remained in seclusion, and I tried not to judge the monastery as a whole by this single, albeit repeated, scene. Still the confrontation with undisciplined minds was nerve jangling and it took some of the zest out of mealtimes, which were otherwise beautiful rituals in my day. I mentioned the disturbances as politely as I could to Sunno as I sipped tea with him. Sunno looked thoughtful, as if searching for the proper explanation for me. "You see, this place has many functions. It is a school for the young monks, and a preaching place for the laymen, so Maha Thera had this meditation section built separately." He said that the young monks were often a distraction to his meditation as well. We talked then for the first time about his own meditation practice and difficulties he was having. I was a little surprised at his naivete toward the whole process, so I offered to lend him some of my books. I thought he might find in them explanations for much of what he found confusing.

He accepted and promised to pay me a visit one afternoon at teatime when he had finished the books so we could continue our discussion. Finally Sunno excused himself to attend a class in the main courtyard.

I headed back over the hill, walking more quickly than usual, and when I reached the hut my heart was pounding and I felt vaguely feverish. My mind was racing. Suddenly I was aware that it had been days and days since I'd said a word to anyone. It took me a few hours to recover from my departure from silence.

When I left America it had always been my intention to return. If people asked, I usually said that I'd be back in the spring.

P and I were never able to talk very much about it because it seemed to upset us both, and dealing with the reality of separating for six months or more was hard enough. When she drove me to the airport she had cried. Neither of us thought we were saying good-bye, but we both were aware of a farewell, and we knew that when we did meet again the circumstances would be different than they ever had been. How, we didn't know. And although we agreed beforehand that letter-writing while being more than ten thousand miles apart was no medium for evolving a relationship, our letters soon turned from news reports to tentative explorations and statements of what we wanted to be to each other. At first I listened, mostly. For the first few months of the journey, although P was never far from my mind's alternating images of fear, love, desire, anger, and tenderness, I was too engulfed by the strange new intensity of discovering my mind to even conceptualize the details of our future together, beyond the simple fantasy of having her in my arms again.

For her too, the first months were a very begin-all-over time of exploring singleness, self-reliance, her face in the mirror. She shared a lot of this with me in loving, well-wishing letters that said without words that she still considered me her closest friend. Then I began moving around to Burma, back to India, down to Ceylon, and her forwarded letters kept missing me by a day or two. A month and a half went by without news from her. When I finally did get a letter, I felt an enormous change. I felt it literally. I couldn't ever recall the exact words, only the heavy, numb feeling, first in my hand and then in my whole body, as I stared at the tissue-thin aerogram.

I showed the letter to a friend, one of the women who was part of the group that had gone with me to Burma, and she couldn't understand my reaction. It sounded to her like P was doing fine. I was unconvinced. My body was telling me something that I couldn't dismiss as a concoction of the mind. I could hear something not expressed in her words, and the message was clear: It's not us anymore, we're separate. I'm here and you're there. The implications of this weren't clear. It didn't seem that she had faced them yet at all.

The months that followed contained more than a few anxious visits to the post office in various locales. My anxieties weren't put to rest by the next change in her tone, cheerful and distant. I felt helpless. When I wrote to her, somewhat complaining about her withdrawal, her reply was defensive, and a little angry. She wrote that I shouldn't judge her from a particular mood she may have been in that one time, especially since she had written other letters which apparently had been lost in forwarding. That only made it worse. Now I knew that she knew that I knew . . . and the distances of time and space were too great for us to be really open with each other. When I left Colombo to head for the monastery the first time, I resolved to let it go. There was nothing I could do now. Letters were not going to ease my mind.

Sometimes I asked myself what I wanted, and I didn't know. It felt like I was simply reacting. Watching her moves, her explorations, and feeling hurt by them. When I thought about it rationally, I knew I didn't want to return to the situation we had had together, marriage without real commitment, a habitual holding on to each other as we struggled with our separate paths.

But the feelings for her were always there. Love and attachment. Sometimes I could clearly distinguish between the two. More often, though, it was simple longing for this person who had shared so much with me. Whose presence, no matter how hard it was for me to handle, was still that familiar extension of my own being that made the universe less formidable, less lonely. Leaving my friends in India, arriving in Ceylon by myself, and finally finding a situation where days would go by without so much as a word to another person, this loneliness and longing for her became by far the most difficult mood of my mind to bear. Sometimes, in the morning when the air was cool and bright and breakfast was sitting in my belly as I walked contentedly with a light step back up the hill to my hut, I could look quite clearly at the desire and see it as just a crystalization of the deep, nameless human fear of our aloneness. I *knew* at those instants that I was alone, that I had been born alone, was alone right now, and at the very last moment, would depart all by myself. And then, as I would stand on my favorite ledge overlooking the monastery courtyard below and look out beyond it to the checkerboard of rice paddies that stretched to the hills, then that aloneness was right, it was perfect, it was real.

But morning became evening. Dusk would grab me with a message of fear, and my aloneness would become a fact that I wasn't so ready to bear. I wanted her presence, her warmth. Often, as I sat sipping my evening tea, listening to the forest come alive with the sounds of the creatures who claimed the night for themselves, floods of memories would overcome me. I would feel myself slipping from the moment, unable to simply observe the tightness in my chest, the thickness in my throat. Why did it have to be this way? Why did we need so much? And then in that pain a new kind of clarity arose. I saw there in the deepest part of my being the terror of being alone.

But P couldn't alter my condition. No matter how much I demanded of her, even if she succeeded, I would still be alone.

One evening, as the collective weight of the experience in this monastery and the months that preceded it seemed to gather in a single moment, I felt a snapping, a cracking of the hold that I'd always had on her. And as it broke both of us were freed of an enormous burden. I understood that what I had always wanted most from her, the end of my aloneness, would never be there, because it didn't exist. In her or in anyone.

So as I finished my tea I knew it was time for a letter. I wrote that I loved her. As best I could, I expressed the love, the affection, and the good feeling that arose whenever I thought of her. Whether we lived together or apart when I returned didn't matter. Our relationship would be different. I was different. There wasn't much more to say until I returned in a month or so. I mailed the letter the day I left the monastery on my visit to Kandy.

About a week after I saw the two monks in their quarters, I was finishing my meal one lunchtime when the boy who served my food told me that Maha Thera was ill. He hadn't been in his familiar chair on the porch that morning at breakfast when I stopped by for my daily blessing, so I went out there to see him now. He giggled when he saw me and blew his nose, as if to say, "What a foolish contraption these bodies are." He knew no English and I, only a few words of Ceylonese but he conveyed the fact that he was doing okay, considering his fever and running nose. Then he grabbed me by the arm and led me over to the site of the new teaching hall that was being built. Each day he stood out there under his parasol personally supervising the construction. Michael, the anthropologist, told me that Maha Thera had come to this site some thirty years ago when it was just a forest and had planned and overseen the building of everything there as well as numerous other hermitages in the country. It was hard to keep a hammer out of his hands. One day Michael, who spoke excellent Ceylonese, asked the old monk why he spent all his time on these projects. Maha Thera had had a formidable reputation for austerities and meditation in his younger days. Now he just played foremen. "Why?" Michael asked, telling him that these buildings on which he spent so much time would be rubble in twenty years. Maha Thera just giggled at the question, Michael told me, then looked around to see if anyone could hear. "Because," he whispered, "it's fun."

Now I looked at him as he put on his stern face to admonish the workmen to take care. He was the real thing, this old boy. He might appear as slack as the chattering gang that hung out in the courtyard, but his eyes gave him away. *He knew what was going on.* I smiled appreciatively at the progress of the construction. Then he bit his lip and made a gesture of suddenly remembering something. He bustled off to his room and returned with a letter addressed to me here at the monastery. My hand was trembling as he gave it to me. It was from my wife.

I only got halfway back up the hill before I sat down and

read it. Just the feel of it in my hand was growing too heavy. Then I returned to the hut and slowly read it again. It was a reply to the letter I had mailed when I left for Kandy. She was overwhelmed, frightened. My profession of love was more than she could handle. She wasn't capable of such love. Word of my return threw her into turmoil. She hadn't thought I would be returning so soon. What did I mean? Would we live together again? She didn't think we could.

Reading the letter was like sitting in a small rowboat in the middle of a lake and watching it sink from a leak that I couldn't reach. First anger and frustration rose around me, and then helplessness at not being able to stop them. What did she mean, *what did I mean?* How could it not be clear? My mind was shuddering as it bore the full impact of her fear. My quiet, confident, loving sense of her was seized with shivering doubts. I was bombarded with images of a long, painful confrontation with her when we met again, and my love deteriorated into exhaustion and resentment.

My resentment felt dreadful, like some disease spreading through my body. I'd been so healthy, so well, and was suddenly furious at this intrusion. What was the letter even doing in my hand, here in this perfect solitude? I got up and walked around the hut perhaps for an hour, beset by images of returning to her, trying to convince, to plead, to placate, to prove something.

I wanted no part of it. My love for her was no fantasy these past weeks. But whether it was because that love was not strong enough to withstand the confrontation with her resistance, or whether it was just the nature of that love to exist here, in silence, alone, I realized that I had no wish to trade that love for desire and frustration.

My reason for returning home now had evaporated. Whether I became ordained a monk or not didn't matter either. I could stay here for as long as I liked. If I really loved her, then that would be enough. I was here and she was there, and the love remained.

I looked around at my hut again. Certain improvements

came to mind. Better lighting. A little work on the grounds. Fix up a cooking stove. I was ready to make it my home.

Sunno never paid his promised visit to my hut for tea. Finally, I went to see him after lunch to at least get my books back. He said that it had proved more difficult than he had thought to get away to visit my place, and when I asked him whether the books had been of any help to him, he answered that while they had seemed very interesting, he had not had time to finish them. "Too much other reading to do, for these classes, you know," he explained.

There didn't seem to be much more to say and I would have left it at that but he asked me to stay and have tea. Not just out of politeness. He was trying to put something into words. "I have to start meditating here soon," he finally said, looking at me with a mixture of pain and relief on his face. I asked him what was stopping him. "I have no time," he replied with the smile of a little boy delivering the punch line to a joke. In fact it was a confession, which, once made, broke the seals that restrained all confidences. When I asked him what took up his time, he recited in exasperation his daily schedule, punctuating the hours with expressions of disbelief at his own predicament. "Four hours a day I spend in classes, learning Pali and Sanskrit and the texts, then I have to spend as much time doing the homework. Then I must teach a class in English to the little *bhikkus*. Then I have to learn the chants. So I have from four until six in the morning for meditation."

I knew he wanted more from me than sympathy for his plight. "What do you mean you 'have to,' Sunno?"

"That is what they expect of me," he answered, as if parroting what he had been told. "There is a proper kind of monk whom they wish to produce here to go and start other places like this."

"And is that what you want to be?"

He almost giggled. "No, of course not. I came here for meditation, really. That is why I left everything in London."

"Then why don't you do it?" I asked. "There is that teacher of meditation, here is the place."

"The teacher," he repeated bemusedly, "Pandita Thera, has meditated very little in his life." I was shocked. I had been introduced to this older monk with bright, twinkling eyes, and we had talked about meditation and he showed me what he had written about it. I asked Sunno about the book. "Yes, yes the book. All he knows is from books. He has spent his whole life as a teacher in places like this, so now he retired and came here to do his own meditation, and what have they done? They make him teach more classes here so he has no time for meditation."

"But why are you doing all this?" I asked angrily.

He shrugged. "I don't know. I can't understand why they have me do this. I don't want to be a teacher. I came here to meditate."

"Then you'll have to leave here to meditate," I said harshly, without even considering what that might mean. I was shocked by my own anger with this place. "Why don't you go to a real meditation center. Where you can find a teacher. Here it will never happen. You can't begin meditation by doing it for an hour or two a day with all these distractions."

"You are right," he said, shaking his head. "I don't know what I'm doing here. I must move up the hill to one of the *kutis*. Here in this place no one meditates. It is a joke, it is called the meditation section, but we all sit around with no teacher."

We talked some more and he admitted that he wasn't happy here, that he had not found what he had given up his life in London for. He expressed his fear that his growing discouragement would cause him to leave without giving the monastic life a chance.

"Sunno, listen. It is very, very hard to begin meditation. That is why Goenka has these camps where all the facilities are designed to help. There is silence, and everyone is doing the same thing, and no other activities are going on. You need that kind of structure to begin. Here there is none of that. The only structure here is the priesthood. It's like a job."

"It is very funny," he mused. "I had a wonderful career in London and I gave it up, just for another?"

"Then leave this one!"

"But that is not so easy."

I turned away and occupied myself with my tea. We had talked long enough. I felt enormously frustrated and even guilty, but I didn't want to be angry with him, because he was basically such a well-intentioned human being. What held him back then? I watched him walk off, still pondering, still wondering.

I walked silently out of Sunno's room through the walled inner courtyard, full of a furious sense of betrayal. Nobody meditated here. I'd been told a lie. This forest hermitage was nothing more than a glorified clubhouse for social dropouts. I heard the gong sound for five o'clock tea. When I entered the meal area through which I had to cross to reach the path leading up the hill, I found the usual crew of young monks hanging around the dining hall. Probably been there since lunch, I thought to myself. Their mindless, smiling faces annoyed the hell out of me. Why don't you sit and watch your minds? I felt like shouting. None of them spoke English. Not until Sunno would teach them. I felt their stares as I walked away from them with my eyes down. I was the strange one here, I thought; I meditated.

By the time I got back to my hut I was ready to pack my bags. I couldn't believe that I had considered spending the rest of my life in this place. I flopped down on my bed, exhausted. The world looked to me then like nothing but a distraction. I wanted to get as far away from it as possible. I decided that the next morning I would speak to Maha Thera, and tell him that I wanted to leave. I needed more solitude than this place afforded. I knew that he had set up other monasteries in the country. Perhaps he could send me to one where I'd find what I was looking for. A cave or maybe just a small house, alone in a tiny village where nobody spoke English.

I went down the hill at midmorning the next day hoping to find Maha Thera. When I reached the inner courtyard, I stopped. The doors were open to the passageway leading out to the main courtyard and through them I saw a long procession. It seemed as if all the monks in the monastery were walking across the yard, in unison, single file with heads down, begging bowls in hand, chanting in time to their steps. They were returning from alms round, the daily ritual of collecting food for the noon meal from the neighboring populace. Near the front of the line was one of the young monks whose silly, laughing presence had often annoyed me most. Now his movement and that of the others crossing the courtyard with powerful, even steps was magnificent. I stood in a trance watching. There was a tranquility, a stillness to their movement that was almost unbearable to me in the state of mind I was in.

I didn't know what to do with the scene, though I felt that there was a lesson here just for me. It was the first time since shortly after my arrival that I had witnessed any of the monastery's formal activities. I knew that I had witnessed something very powerful and religious, in a sense I had not known before. A group exercise in awareness and humility. A meditation. When all the monks had passed, I proceeded outside to look for Maha Thera.

He was seated on the porch of his quarters in his familiar place that gave him a good view of the comings and goings in the central courtyard. He greeted me with the tickled look of glee I always got from him and muttered his blessing as I prostrated at his feet. *"Bhawana?"* he asked sharply as he folded his hands in his lap in mock solemnity. It was the Pali word for meditation, and he wanted a report on my progress in sitting. But before I could even answer, he looked into my eyes and shook his head, making little tsk-tsk sounds. Then he sent for someone to translate for us. As we were waiting he slapped his knee, chortling and muttering to himself. He called me to his side, and from under a mound of papers he pulled out a cardboard-bound notebook and handed it to me. At first I didn't understand. Then I remembered that a week ago I'd asked Sunno if one of the laymen who attended the monastery could get me a new notebook. Now Maha Thera was laughing and making scribbling gestures in the air saying, "Good, good."

When our translator arrived I immediately began to state my case. I realized I was criticizing my host indirectly by asking to leave, but I felt sure that Maha Thera would understand, because I'd heard many times the stories of his early years when he set off alone for forests and caves to practice the most intensive type of solitary meditation. But the more I explained, the more he stared at my eyes and shook his head in disappointment.

He didn't answer immediately. He had one eye all along on the activities around us. It was nearing lunchtime. Suddenly, before he could say anything, a huge crowd of well-dressed laypeople appeared at the top of the entrance steps at the far end of the courtyard. They were apparently visitors from the city, here for a day, almost as a tour group, to feed the monks, nose around the grounds, and receive the teachings from the *bhikkus*. I panicked and began excusing myself to try to make a run for my hut. Maha Thera insisted I stay. He asked me to go on with what I had to say, but I could hardly speak. The next thing I knew the visitors were crowded around the porch paying their respects to the old monk and gawking at me. I felt a nauseous heat rising through my body, as if their ordinary, workaday city minds were all inside my head. I didn't even dare look at the women. Maha Thera, unperturbed, smiled and calmly received his visitors' well wishes. He seemed neither condescending nor particularly solicitous toward them. He remained his stern, grandfatherly self.

When he introduced me as a young man who was here for serious meditation practice, I almost went through the floor. The visitors seemed impressed, and one of them began asking me polite questions about my stay in the monastery. I could barely talk. I felt dizzy. Then I felt angry, just as angry as I had been when I put P's letter down. Why couldn't they just leave me alone? I looked at the man's face. I had nothing to say to him. He seemed like an unrecognizable entity. As I stood there staring, Maha Thera began giggling hysterically. Then he shook his head, *"Bhawana, bhawana . . .* tsk, tsk, tsk." Boy, he was saying, you've been sitting with your eyes closed for too long. Then he said something to our translator, who repeated, "Maha Thera wants to know, when you go off to some cave, what will you have to say to the person who gives you your food?"

The old monk had been playing with me this morning. I suddenly recalled how hard it had been to get him to permit me to move out from the central complex to my secluded hut. At that time, although Sunno had suggested I take food with me, Maha Thera had insisted that I come down twice a day for my meals. It was because he didn't want me to isolate myself as much as I did that he had summoned me to attend the initiation ceremony a few days after my arrival. He wanted me to see and even participate a little in what was going on here. Now he seemed to be saying, "See, look what a mess you've made of yourself out there."

But I suddenly realized it was not a total loss. I had taken an excursion of the mind that had been profitable in many ways. I had no regrets. The parts of my mind I had seen and the things I had learned would never have been accessible to me in any other way. But now I was trying to make a way of life out of that excursion. My effort was not to see into phenomena but to avoid those circumstances that caused the reactions of my mind that I found uncomfortable.

My cave was a fantasy. When you are alone for so long it is easy to make believe that you are holy and high. Then whatever disturbs you is a distraction. Desire and fear and anger haven't been overcome, just avoided. In the cave there's not much to remind you who you really are. That's what this horde of tourists was doing here, keeping everyone on their toes. I could see that in everyone's face. Of course, this monastery was full of distractions. Living with others is a distraction. A distraction from stillness. But stillness is just stillness. Somehow, though, I had elevated it to a goal, an end in itself.

It was time for me to go home. It was time for me to face

my mind. This really wasn't the place for me. For the residents of the monastery, being a monk, teaching among the people, begging for alms had gut meaning. There weren't even any other Americans here to remind me of my past. The past can't be cut off by avoidance. Did I really believe that it would be all over with P if I simply never saw her again and dwelt in that distance, believing in an abstract love I could manifest with my eyes closed? I would have to see her again. For what purpose, I couldn't say, except to explore whatever it was that had kept us so bound to each other all these years, and was pushing me to a cave right now.

I was so out of touch. I didn't particularly want to get back in touch, and the idea of actually confronting P, of trying to work things out, if anything could be worked out, brought a wave of exhaustion over my mind. But I had to. It was time to turn the boat around.

Three days later my bags were packed and I was saying goodbye. I was amazed at how hard it turned out to be. Maha Thera was perfectly understanding, but a little sigh said he was sad to see me go. I saved Sunno for last. At his place in the meditation center, he came out to greet me. We stood silently for a moment. There was something, it seemed, that he had to to say. "You are lucky," he began, "to be born an American. Not for the material reason, but because of your outlook, your energy. After being here for a while, I realized that for the Ceylonese this spiritual business is very hard. They are lazy, lazy because they think they have so much time. Endless lifetimes. So they do a little now, and store up merit for the future. They are so willing to say that it is their *karma* that they are not suited for the work of meditation. The next lifetime they say."

"Sunno," I said, "my American teacher, Hover, told us a story. The Buddha explained to his followers that to appreciate how fortunate they are to have been born as human beings capable of understanding and practicing the *dharma*, they should imagine that somewhere in all the oceans of the world there is a great blind sea turtle, and somewhere else, an ox yoke is thrown into the waters. Once a century the blind turtle pokes his head through the surface of the water. How long it takes that turtle to poke his head through the yoke as they float along, that is how long it takes us to be born again as humans."

Sunno smiled. "But you see, sooner or later the turtle will put his head through that yoke. Time is endless, what is the difference? That is what the people in my country understand. You don't understand that, or if you do, it doesn't really affect you. You come halfway around the world to meditate. In London I had that kind of energy. Here it is fading."

I just nodded. We shook hands for the first time. It was not something these monks ordinarily did. I loved Sunno. It was impossible not to. His goodness was impeccable. "Goodbye," I finally said. "Be happy, I wish you the best, always."

"You have your work to do," he said as I turned to go. "You know that."

His words stayed with me. A strange thought, *lucky to be an American*. The energy. Running around the world to get enlightened. Sitting and sitting, alone in a forest. And then finding that I had to return home. Right then the most amazing thing of all about this meditation process was that I could act without understanding the rationale and yet I could have faith in the intuition that the action was right. So as I got back on the bus, I realized that I was going home not because it made sense, but because it felt right.

13

The Essence is Anicca

THE TWO-BLADED FAN above my head cut ponderously through the thick, hot air. It was late April and the annual three-month heat wave was in full bloom in Madras. My own body temperature had gone amok with some indeterminate fever, and I'd spent the past three days in this hotel room waiting quietly for my illness to pass. It was a comfortable enough place to be sick, with its clean, white walls and stone floors, and outside, a balcony that overlooked gardened courtyards where huge trees reached up to the third tier of rooms. The dark and faintly musky atmosphere was almost Mediterranean.

I sat up and waited for the room to stop swirling. Then I greedily gobbled down a handful of vitamin C tablets and, with more restraint, a couple of bananas. God, it would be so easy to simply go home. I could be in Boston the day after tomorrow. End the suspense, just be there. And see what the next chapter is all about. What I was doing now certainly made no sense. Fighting my way back all the way up to Calcutta in hundred-plus degree heat to spend all my money on six and a half more days of meditation when I'd just done six months of it. Back to Burma. I'd told them I'd be back when I left. Back for what? What did they have to teach me now?

I stretched out on the bed again, aware that I really didn't want to go back to Burma, yet I was doing it. Those two weeks there back in January had been crucial, perhaps the crucial event of this trip. But that was past. Their lessons had been learned. And my stay in the forest in Ceylon had taught me that you can't go on repeating the same lessons. All the same, there was something I had to know, something only they could tell me. That experience, that moment that I still could not describe, the moment when my mind stopped, it had occurred again more than once since that morning alone in my hut. Was it *nirvana*? I had to know whether it was, because that was the only way I could know what I might be. And only they could tell me.

It was well into evening when I finally made my way through customs at the Rangoon airport. I tried to call the International Meditation Center but got no answer. I knew that someone should be there because this was the time for their retreat that coincided with the Burmese new year. I also knew that they closed the front gate at night. So I jumped into a cab and told the driver it was worth five extra *khyats* if he got me there before nine. I hoped I would be welcome. I had written U Chit Tin a letter from Colombo a while back but had received no reply.

When I arrived the gate was still open and a light was on in the discourse hall at the top of the hill. I trundled with my bags up the long stairway and was startled to find Sayama, her husband, U Chit Tin, and several others whom I recognized seated around the table sipping tea. They nodded casually as I came in as if they were expecting me. "The plane arrived late this evening," U Chit Tin remarked. "Come in, come in, would you like some tea and fruit?" Sayama herself brought out bananas, sliced papaya, and pineapple. I started at her flat-cheek-boned, pale face, rimmed by her still dark hair pulled tightly back. Her age was not apparent. I saw both a girl and a grand-mother. Her eyes were neither penetrating nor evasive. They were just there. When she handed me the fruit she laughed. Not a giggle, but a hearty backslapping laugh. As usual, I was at a loss in her presence. I turned to U Tint Yee and he smiled, almost shyly. Suddenly I remembered how much this man, the soft-spoken chairman who commanded so much silent respect from the others, had meant to me on my first visit here. Our minds had so powerfully connected the last time; his lessons had been so lasting. I watched him calmly relight his cigar. His movements were spare, economical. Precision flowed naturally from him.

"We saved a room for you," U Chit Tin said with a feigned matter-of-factness that let me know that kind attention was being lavished upon me. "We got your letter. You didn't re-ceive my reply? Ah, the mail here. But I knew you'd be here tonight." He said it so firmly that I wondered how I had been so unsure all week.

"So," asked U Ba Pho, the secretary, the "ambassador" I might have called this well-tailored man with long black hair combed straight back, cigarette in hand and perfect English at his command. "Tell us of your trip."

And then, until it was so late that we all were nearly falling asleep, I told them about Ceylon and the monastery, and my meeting with Nyanaponika, and my plans for scholarly books and papers I hoped to write, and my friends, *Bhikkus* Sunno and Ratanapala, and their attempts at meditation. I listened as they told me about other groups of Westerners who had come to the center, of news of my friends back in India, and of their own health and doings. It was hard not to tell them what I *really* wanted to report. I dropped some hints about my medita-tion practice, but I knew that would have to wait. I was happy though; I loved these people. It felt wonderful just to be in their presence and I felt the magic in the place more strongly than when I'd been there before. "It feels like coming home," I finally said. U Chit Tin smiled and nodded appreciatively. It would be a fine week.

The next day I sat quietly in my cell staring at the little light at the end of my nose. At teatime when U Chit Tin asked me how the day's sitting had gone, I thought, "Finally, I'll get to tell him the whole story." But as soon as I described the light, he cut me off, consulted with Sayama, and informed me that I was to leave the light alone, and begin with *vipassana* meditation immediately. Wonderful, I thought, they recognize my state of advancement. Only one day watching the breath alone instead of the usual three and now on to the real thing. The following day at lunch I cornered U Chit Tin outside the dining hall and began telling him what had happened in Ceylon. Almost immediately his attention froze into a wall, his eyes turned to mirrors, and my words bounced off his mind. He didn't want to hear what I had to say. "Enough," he held up a hand. "Too much talk, save it for Sayama."

That afternoon in my cell, the experience of the state of all mind stopping occurred again. I could hardly wait for the end of the hour to tell Sayama about it. At teatime I asked U Chit Tin to deliver my request for a interview with her. He nodded somberly and said I could come into the hall after the last meditation of the evening.

When I emerged from my cell, it was dark as I made my way to the discourse hall. Removing my shoes at the door I entered to find nearly my entire welcoming committee at the table. I quietly took a seat and waited until I could see Sayama privately. But U Chit Tin asked me quite directly what I had to say. The teachers were all silent as I described my experience of that afternoon. I had been sitting watching the sensations in my body when, after a time, my concentration deepened and I was just aware of rapid dissolution, like rain falling on a lake. As the phenomenon increased in speed, my mind grew steadier, more focused, and I became aware of my mind itself as it registered the phenomenon in my body. Then my awareness of the mind process grew more rapid as well until suddenly the sensation in the body was completely quiet, like still water, until only awareness of the mind remained. I watched the bubble of mind formations until suddenly the mind simply clicked off.

"That's what I experienced in Ceylon as well," I added. U Tint Yee translated for Sayama, but she didn't seem to be listening. She was staring directly at me. Her eyes, as wide as saucers, transfixed me. When U Tint Yee finished, Sayama spoke a few quick words and then slapped the table with the palm of her hand. There was silence around her. She pounded the table once or twice with her fist to punctuate her loud singsong Burmese repeating a few phrases at the end of quick, decisive sentences. I didn't recognize a word she said, but I knew the meaning of what she was saying. The force of it laid me back in my chair. I had always thought of Sayama as a figurehead, a symbol of the real teaching authority of the men. Now it was clear that the men were looking to her for an answer they could not provide. U Tint Yee asked a few questions for clarification, it seemed. Sayama's reply was emphatic and insistent. I looked at U Tint Yee's face as he prepared to translate what Sayama had said. The flesh on his high cheekbones tensed and his lips pursed. In a quiet modulated voice he told me "Sayama says that you must continue to observe the sensations in the body. Over and over again. Maintain your awareness of *anicca*, not this quietness."

Wait a minute, you didn't hear me right! I wanted to scream, but I couldn't even open my mouth, as Sayama gazed at me with curious indifference. Finally she stared off into space and I repeated my story, emphasizing what seemed to have been overlooked.

When I finished, Sayama spoke quickly again. I braced myself instinctively against her words and listened to Tint Yee's translation of her description of the *signs* one manifests before the nirvanic state. I struggled to portray them, but knew I couldn't. Then I became furious. How could it be just that way? How could she know? I stared directly into Sayama's calm, almost sleepy eyes and the pit of my stomach dropped through my feet as my body sagged in the chair. She was staring right through me. I had no idea what she saw but she knew. I knew what she knew. And when she knew that I accepted that, she chuckled and looked away. My brain teetered toward collapse.

U Chit Tin had been silent so far. At one point he had gotten up from the table with a weary look on his face. He was the one I was closest to, we shared an interest in texts and ideas, and he had become almost like a father to me. He seemed pained by this whole discussion.

"You have been diverted," he said to me now, almost comfortingly, and then he added, "it happened that way to us, too." A little smile must have crossed my lips. As I sighed the heavy atmosphere in the room dissipated.

U Ba Pho ran his fingers through his long black hair. "You are in the vicinity, but you haven't hit the bullseye."

"When you lose the sensation in the body," U Tint Yee added, "when it goes to this 'quietness' that you describe, that is because your concentration has dropped and you are no longer perceiving the sensations, no longer aware of *anicca*. The awareness of *anicca* must not be lost. That awareness must be maintained. It is the whole practice." Then he described precisely, almost like a technician, what must be done to keep the mind alert, aware of *anicca*, and how to focus the awareness to a greater and greater intensity.

When he finished there was silence. Sayama said something else, then got up and left first. We hadn't really exchanged eye contact once. My mind felt like an empty water bag. I watched the last few proud drops of my spiritual achievement drip out on the floor. Then I felt empty indeed. Chastised, put in my place, and not a little bit foolish.

"A *jhanic* state, trance," U Tint Yee commented. "You have built up very strong concentration, so it was easy for it to stick to an object, the wrong object. You stopped being aware of *anicca*. Only the awareness, uninterrupted awareness of *anicca* takes you to that moment of the unconditioned. When you experienced that quietness you lost the awareness of impermanence and strayed into the trance state."

I had lost awareness, and insight, and had begun diving into some very pleasant, joyous state of *samadhi*, deep, one-pointed concentration. I laughed. It was so clear now why I had returned to Burma, though I'd been fighting coming here all the way. That's what that fever in Madras had been about. I was carrying something here, something I was afraid might get stolen. Some precious burden that I wanted to sneak through customs: my accomplishment, my spiritual certificate of achievement. All the more valuable because I earned it myself. Without these precious gurus. Then why did I come here? Or rather, how had I gotten here?

I sat still at the table. My mind was still humming from Sayama's words. My self-image was rubble. I sat on the pile and my entire mind-body felt clear of all the feverishness of the past few weeks. Incredibly, I felt good. Completely defeated, my achievement wiped out, and good. Sayama had just kicked the stool out from under me and the ground felt wonderful.

The next day I set out to get back on the track that I'd fallen off of in Ceylon: to really accomplish what I had set out to do, to experience this wholly other state of mind, *nirvana*. Absolute freedom; a state beyond even what I had reached, mere realms of trance. It appeared to me that I was close, and I was cheerfully confident that in the four remaining days I could get there. After breakfast I met U Tint Yee and once again, in his quietly intense way, he explained the pitfalls and the way to that moment of absolute one-pointedness and insight that opened the gate to the unconditioned state. U Tint Yee's manner conveyed his teaching even more than his words. By treating my dramatic quest for liberation in a matter-of-fact technical manner he repeated each time, "Stop thinking, stop worrying, stop looking ahead. Simply do this. Concentrate on this. Apply your attention to this. And let the results come on their own." I steadied my mind, searching for the signs that matched the teacher's descriptions.

When I left U Tint Yee, I sat for three hours without moving. I felt so frustratingly close to the state I sought that I barely ate anything for lunch. After resting for only a few minutes, I was back in my cell where I sat for another hour before the spasm began in my gut. For the rest of the afternoon I lay on my side in the darkened cell, trying to sail over the waves of shooting pain that tore at my intestines in increasingly shorter intervals by riveting my attention on my breath. When the pain became overwhelming, I would bite my handkerchief to keep from screaming. Every hour I tiptoed outside, trying not to arouse the demons in my body until I could expel them over the toilet.

The next day the diarrhea continued but the spasm subsided enough to continue the quest. Sayama warned me to go slower or I might not be able to bear the results. I could only agree. I stuck to watching the sensations in my body without being pulled into them, but by late afternoon I distinctly felt my attention being drawn deeper within. The body became quiet but that substanceless point that U Tint Yee had spoken of was there, and as my attention sought its handle, my mind seemed to explode in bursts of light, while goose flesh rippled over my body. My attention was totally distracted by these events and I couldn't regain it. But now at least, I knew I was really close.

At the evening break when I blurted out to Sayama what had happened, her response left me silent. "Stop trying for that event. Just stay with the sensations only, observing them over and over. Keep cleaning, keep cleaning. There is more to do." What do you mean more to do? I felt like shouting. I heard U Chit Tin vaguely in the background repeating the instructions. *Keep cleaning, there is more to do*, until his words were drowned out by the roar of my inner dialogue. *Clean what? I'm ready. I tell you.* And then a weird chill ran up my spine as I glanced at Sayama and *knew* that she was aware of my response. She sat there perfectly quiet, her brows knitted slightly, a look of weary patience on her face, as if under some great burden. I felt as though I'd been staring into a deep luminous glass, until I saw my own reflection. My mind was still. She had silenced my argument.

Then U Chit Tin abruptly changed the subject. "You are lucky to be here now, these five days," he said. "These are the days of the course U Ba Khin gave for us each year, and tonight, Sunday, is the special night when the *forces* are strongest."

Once again that word which had entered our conversation more and more these days had a jarring, unsettling effect on my mind. I looked up at him. He was smiling, but the air of seriousness in the shrine room where we three were seated on the wooden floor was unmistakable. I found myself staring at the huge photograph of U Ba Khin seated in a meditative pose, and then back at Sayama. It took an enormous effort, but I asked him if he could explain what he meant by these forces.

"There are other beings," he began, "in the other planes of existence—*Brahmas* and *Devas* above us, and in terms of the span of their lifetimes, the *Nirvana Dhatu* that the Buddha brought forth is still new, still fresh. Twenty-five hundred years is like a day or less to them, and there it lives, fresh and alive, and they are just waiting to bestow it on those that can receive it."

Then they sent me back downstairs to my cell with a final reminder of this coming hour's significance. Sunday evening of this course was probably the most powerful sitting of the year. I had no idea what that meant, but I was filled with a new anticipation. I had first heard the words *Nirvana Dhatu* at the end of our visit here back in February when we entered the cells facing the central shrine room to pay our respects and receive Sayama's blessing. She had us begin meditating and then directed our attention to the top of our heads to receive this *Nirvana Dhatu*. It had felt as though liquid electricity was being poured through my body. The sensation lasted for days afterwards. What was it? At one point U Chit Tin had said that it was the same as *anicca*. That is, when you truly experience *anicca*, then you are experiencing the *Nirvana Dhatu*.

I pulled the door to my cell closed and slipped the bolt. Immediately I noticed the difference in the air, and this only added to my resolve. I actually believed that this would be the hour, that I was ready and the spark would be kindled. For the first half hour, though, the only sparks I managed were caused by the friction of my struggle to keep my attention where I wanted it. Each time I dragged it back the heat rose, until finally the explosion occurred. It suddenly felt as if huge weights had been dropped on my shoulders. My whole body sagged, and then began to squirm under the load. I tried to sit up straight but couldn't, and then I felt the weight accumulate on my neck, pressing my body down, bending it at the waist. My head was dropping to the floor as I struggled to right myself. I felt the weight growing, becoming some enormous, undeniable presence in my whole body. I was fighting, for an unknown reason, to keep my forehead from touching the floor, until the struggle exhausted me and slowly, inch by inch, my torso continued to bend until my brow rested on the hardwood floor. At that instant an image came roaring out of the blackness of my mind: a seated figure, calm and imperturbable. I recognized the image as the photograph of U Ba Khin in the shrine room, was relieved by the recognition, then lost all sense of having-seen-before as the flat, photographic image developed itself into something with substance, three-dimensional, alive and radiating energy, no longer at a distance but visible, right within me. And then my body began to rise, without any effort of mine. My shoulders still felt heavy. I was upright but slumping, like a rag doll propped up against a tree, only it was the contents of my mind, that image of the Teacher, that held me aloft, kept me up and blasted open for the remainder of the hour.

On the fifth evening as we sat once again in the central shrine room of the pagoda, U Chit Tin made a remark that I had heard before, "Sayama says you were better the first time you came." I had told him and the others about the presence of U Ba Khin the night before and the strange events of this past day. Sitting had become increasingly difficult and the weight on my shoulders returned. I struggled through an hour, but by the end of it I was bent over and sobbing, deep shuddering sobs that had no source except the bottomless insubstantiality that my attention was rooted to. I had to leave the cell and sit outside. Still the sense of emptiness would not leave, and I felt completely despondent.

"You see," U Chit Tin said, "there are strange forces in places like forests. When you are off alone, Mara, evil, is there with you, just waiting to tempt you off the path, sometimes with hardships but more subtly with some pleasant state or another. Now that force that overcame you is being cleansed and you can see just how strong it is."

Mara, the evil one, the force of negativity. Image of the Buddha seeking enlightenment under the solitary Bodi tree, assaulted by the hosts of Mara in his vigil. Temptations of sensual pleasure, power, immortality. Mythological trappings to the story? No, Mara is real, or at least what Mara represents is real. Mara is right here, built into this process. Mara is the impulse, the almost gravitational pull, to further suffering. The little voice that whispers, "Get up. Don't sit for an hour. It hurts. It hurts too much!" And when you've gotten past that ruse, Mara has subtler and subtler ones. Somewhere out in the solitude of the forest my ego had fought its last stand, and by feigning death had won its survival. It made the compromise that would satisfy us both. The ego would act as though extinguished and I would believe that I had extinguished it. But while I believed my accomplishment, the ego hung on, silent and smiling, willing now to exchange the bruising tactics of confrontation for the more effective method of deception. You have killed your ego, it whispered so quietly, so convincingly that I didn't even question the source. You have fought the battle of solitude and loneliness. You have achieved more than all those devotees who remain tied to Goenka, more than those rote disciples in Burma who will never cut the apron strings of their teacher even though he is dead. You have achieved what they have struggled for all their lives—the place in the stream. You are the streamwinner, the *Sotapanna!* The one who has attained access to *nirvana*.

And it was all my accomplishment. It had nothing to do with my teachers; in fact, it was accomplished more easily without them. The most awesome aspect of understanding this deception, I realized as I sat there looking at U Chit Tin's smile, was the dimension, the apparent bottomlessness of the well of self. I could no longer even pride myself on my ability to penetrate the sham, because that was another layer of sham. I thought about the ease with which one goes from watching to wanting.

Now I was able to watch again, because I had been shown how. The subtle distinction between "working out your own salvation" and believing that it is *you* who is working out your own salvation seemed nearly beyond my comprehension.

That is what they were pointing out to me, beginning with Sayama's assault on my mind. I had never really submitted to her, never accepted the reverence all the others showed toward her. What did she have to teach me? Nothing, except the end of all conceptions. The night she pounded the table and nullified my "accomplishment," she emptied my mind, if only for a moment, of every belief it had. For an instant I had submitted completely to her guidance and protection, because she had destroyed the element of choice. She had revealed a type of power that ended in a single moment my ability to hold her at a distance and decide on her abilities. She had blasted that distance and now I felt her inside me, examining me directly and determining exactly who I was in a way I would never be able to do. She was looking right through me. I knew that the descriptions of my experience that I was offering were unnecessary, that she could somehow judge whether I had "attained" anything or not by simply looking; that is how much she could see. Thus her assessment was nearly unbearable, because there was absolutely no way to dismiss it. I struggled with it, struggled with my self, but she was relentless. The tones she used drilled right through me. How could anybody be so sure? How does she know? Yet she did. I looked at her and knew that I didn't know anything. This middle-aged grandmother who showed more concern about preparing lunch than meditating, who could flip through a comic book while U Chit Tin and I struggled over a point of doctrine, who never bothered to talk when she could laugh, knew it all.

The formal period of my meditation was just about over. I would be leaving Burma the next morning, beginning my journey home. It was still a little hard adjusting to the realization that the trip was ending without the experience that I was so sure I had achieved just a while back. I felt a lingering ambiguity. A lack of certainty about the significance of much that I'd been through. At my last teatime gathering with the teachers I was seeking some clarification. Sayama was not at the table. It was only U Chit Tin, U Ba Pho, Goenka's brother, and myself. U Chit Tin was interested in telling me stories about U Ba Khin but I tried to steer him back to the topic of *nirvanic* experience. I thought I was being subtle. I was looking for an appraisal, a forecast, what I might expect, how far I had to go until I might experience . . .

He knew just what I was fishing for. He smiled and started to clean his glasses. "Do you know what *parami* is?" he asked, almost innocently. I thought I did. It was a technical term for spiritual ability or propensity. When I'd heard it before I thought it meant that some people simply meditated better than others. They had more *parami* just as some people are born more intelligent than others. Somehow just the way U Chit Tin asked me the question made me realize that I didn't understand *parami* completely.

He started talking about "lifetimes," about the process of existence that is beginningless and endless, in which this body, this person whom we recognize as ourselves is nothing but a phase, a passing moment. When Hover had first mentioned it a couple of years ago it hadn't registered at all. Now it made some sense. What I had found deep within this mind and body was a process. The process manifests itself over and over again, birth after birth in endless forms. We aren't a soul or entity that exists and jumps from body to body. We don't transmigrate. We change. We alter moment after moment. We alter, and each lifetime is just another moment of alteration in this stream of energy. The alteration is not random. Randomness is not a characteristic of the universe. The universe is really mind. *Mind precedes all*, the Buddha observed. The mind has purpose, will. The will comes from desire, from hatred, from anger, from delusion. Or the will comes from love, from nonattachment, from wisdom. We become what we will. We are what we have willed. The stream of energy that is endless is a wheel. That is the image of suffering. We turn the wheel with our minds, our minds steeped in delusion and attachment. We come into being, into bodies whose nature is decay and suffering *because* we will that. This is the law of *karma*. Buddha said he was here to teach the end of this suffering, the way off the wheel. *Nirvana* is the end of becoming. It is just being. The body ends and the life energy requires no new body. The chain of birth and death is broken because the mind has been so purified of its attachments that it takes hold of no new form. This is deathlessness.

To get there, I had believed, you sit and you sit and you sit. U Chit Tin smiled at my beliefs as a patient father would at his child's recitation of a fairy tale.

"We cannot comprehend," he said, "the *paramis* that must be developed to achieve that freedom, *parinirvana*. Our suffering is so beginningless . . ." He paused to see if I could even approach that notion. "How long it takes to reverse that, to build up the ability that we must have to get free . . ." He shook his head as if it wasn't even worth imagining. "And also what we must achieve for that," he went on, "is very difficult to comprehend. There are many *paramis*," he said, "in the end we must have them all. Some sit well, very well. They have very deep meditation and it helps them on this path. But there is more, too. We work very hard for this *nirvanic* experience in our meditation, yes? But whether it comes in this lifetime or another, we still must work hard to develop *parami*. We develop giving to others, right conduct, patience, wisdom, loving-kindness. We work for ourselves and for others. Otherwise we do not build our *parami*."

I was aware of how myopic my vision had become, how intense my preoccupation with spiritual achievement. Meditation had no relation to others for me. It was about solitude and loneliness and the confrontation with my mind. Necessary, absolutely necessary, but only a part of this path. "To teach," U Chit Tin told me, "to help others on this path is a very special gift."

Then he began to tell me about his marriage to Sayama. He had known her even when she was a young girl in the town where they lived. Then a local astrologer had predicted to him that his wife would excel him in spiritual matters. For a while U Chit Tin and Sayama were the typical Burmese couple, he a young accountant in government service and she a wife and mother. He had already been meditating under U Ba Khin's tutelage for a few years when he took her to his teacher for a course of instruction. U Chit Tin smiled at me. "In ten days," he snapped his fingers, "she got the whole of the *Dharma*." Afterwards Sayama rarely left U Ba Khin's side when he taught. They moved onto the grounds of the Center, living in separate quarters on the sanctified grounds, and for twenty-five years they served their teacher.

When U Ba Khin died, Sayama nearly despaired. She didn't think she would be able to teach without her guru, and the Center remained closed due both to the political situation in the country and the problems of U Ba Khin's survivors. But now, through no real efforts of their own, it was open once more and they were all busy again, teaching, serving, glad of it. U Chit Tin told me that for a while he had been suffering from high blood pressure, but now it was better. He was doing the most important work of all, giving to others this precious gift, Buddha's Way.

Dana Parami. The Perfection of Giving. Who can willingly make a life's work of serving others? What must be the purity of mind to let go of personal situation and become an instrument to serve others? This as much as *jhana* or unconditioned states is the road to Buddhahood. "We are happy," U Chit Tin concluded. He wasn't particularly looking backward over a lifetime or to what lay ahead. A simple fact of life. Unmistakable. Unlike any expression of satisfaction I'd ever heard anyone use to describe their life. And that was the reason why anyone who visited this place left so much richer than when they arrived. These people could teach you not only how to meditate, but how to live.

U Chit Tin had one more surprise for me. Each evening after tea the Burmese disciples, some twenty or so, gathered in the discourse hall before the great empty chair of the master to listen to tape recordings of his sermons in Burmese. I sat outside, transfixed by the low, resonant voice, wishing the words were available as well. On this last evening, though, I was about to hear the one tape U Ba Khin had recorded in English, a talk called "The Essentials of Buddha *Dharma* in Practice."

"As you sit you must meditate," U Chit Tin instructed me, looking carefully to see if I understood. He seemed almost mischievous, as if bidding me to open my mouth and close my eyes to receive a big surprise. I sat down cross-legged on the floor in front of the Teacher's big, empty chair.

"For progress in *vipassana* meditation, a student must keep knowing *anicca*, impermanence, as continuously as possible," U Ba Khin began. "The continuity of awareness of *anicca* is the secret of success. The last word of the Buddha just before he breathed his last and passed away into the Great, Final *nirvana* was 'Impermanence,' or *anicca*, 'is inherent in all component things. Work out your own salvation with diligence.'"

His words, like Goenka's, I thought, have that unmistakable *power* to disarm, to defuse the mind and penetrate with meaning. Goenka's voice was more dramatic, more theatrical in a way, spellbinding in style. U Ba Khin's is . . . mind clicked off. My little running commentary that accompanied the digestion of his words expired. Now only U Ba Khin and I were left. His voice was deep and reasonable, emitting a rumbling certainty that completely stilled my measurement of his words, his phrases, his ideas.

"In *vipassana* meditation," he said, "one contemplates not only upon the changing nature of matter, but also upon the changing nature of mind, the thought elements projected toward the process of change in matter." As he said it I observed my mind disintegrate. Thought, awareness, consciousness itself was no longer an entity, a solid blob of me. It was a continuum of microscopic events. Like little cartoon thought balloons, popping at a dizzying rate of speed. "You should know also," U Ba Khin informed me," that *anicca* can be understood through other types of feeling as well. By contact of visible form with the sense organ of eye, by contact of sound with the sense organ of ear . . ." Everywhere now. Touch sensation of air against skin, sound of rustling feet against ear, white light flashing against inner eye. *Anicca, anicca anicca.* Reality. I was melting under his words. Be aware, he was pointing. No place in particular to look. It is everywhere. In everything. *Anicca.* The word has no translation anymore. It just is. The perception of things as they are. *Anicca* is a symbol of their essence, their essential nature. Not this, not this, not this. Change alone. What is change? Not "this thing changes." No, the reality is not *this thing,* this tree, this chair, this word, this sound, this idea, this preception. They are not reality. The moment of contact between inner mind and external object is the locus only, while the event that transpires there is *anicca.* Chaaaaaaaaaaaaaaaannn-nnnnnnnnnnnnngggggggggggggge. Chant the word forever, it goes on changing that much longer and longer. Nothing is. Only change.

The tape recorder clicked off. A moment later, I felt a stiffness in my joints that I had been totally unaware of during the forty minutes of U Ba Khin's record talk.

U Chit Tin had on the Cheshire cat's smile when I opened my eyes. I had trouble moving. My body had not yet come together. It felt completely porous. I continued to hear U Ba Khin's voice, no, rather I sensed his presence still. How could the tape capture so much? U Chit Tin and I said little to each other. The message had been clear.

On the morning of my flight back to Calcutta, I received Sayama' blessings in the shrine room. U Chit Tin repeated the Buddha's words to his disciples, "Go ye forth for the good and welfare of all." Then he nodded to Sayama and she reached behind her and handed me a small, marble Buddha statue. Her smile as she handed me the statue was not an indication of mere gracious bestowal but rather a laughing reference to the hard time I'd given her all week. I sighed. No *nirvana*, so I get a statue for a consolation prize. I hadn't given up until the last. Even last night after hearing the tape of U Ba Khin I returned to my cell thinking, "this could be it . . . ."

But it wasn't. Something else was happening. That porous feeling was still with me. I was having a little trouble focusing my attention on objects. Everything kept dissolving. Now as I closed my eyes and listened to Sayama chant her blessings to me, I felt like a neon tube. *Put your attention at the top of your head*, U Chit Tin whispered. I felt illuminated as if I were a glowing light bulb. Slowly I bowed forward until my head touched the floor near her foot. Thank you, Sayama, my heart said. No *Nirvana* but something else, something beyond words. Change, the change in me, I know it, can't say it yet. It is all different now.

"Come," U Chit Tin finally said, "breakfast and then we must be going."

The fork hung midway between plate and mouth as I stared humbly at it. The touch of the silver on my fingers, the weight in my hand, my fingers were like shadows. I bit into the food and was awed as my jaws slowed to a ponderous grinding movement. It was all so amazing. As if the whole movie had been slowed down to a flickering procession of images before me. Nothing had any solidity. Not me, not it. The big melt. Sounds rattled the bones in my ears. My nose trembled under smells. Everything was quivering, pulsing, Everything was alive. Momentary life. My attention couldn't isolate anything. Couldn't freeze anything. Backdrops were collapsing, horizons sinking, points of reference exploding.

Good-byes were formal as always. Just another event. Of course. You're leaving. Safe journey. *U Chit Tin, Sayama, U Tint Yee, I love you all.* Of course, of course, their smiles said. Of course! Don't you understand?

I do. At least I think I do; that is, I don't!

They smiled. Very good.

What's to understand?

Sayama was bustling about, ready to start lunch preparations. U Chit Tin was getting ready to leave for the office. The grandchildren were pedaling around on their tricycles and some women were watering the flower pots. *Explain the mystery of it all, Sayama.* What mystery, she would probably reply.

14

Time Past and Time Present

D<small>ELHI HOT LIKE A KILN</small>. I wandered through empty streets at midday making final connections. London like a plunge into ice water, only hours later. I stood shivering in the transit lounge, my thin wool shawl wrapped tight around my shoulders, my socks incongruous in Indian sandals, even more incongruous in white pajama clothes, amidst fur and leather coats, heavy sweaters and fat, flushed, liquor-stained faces. I was emaciated by comparison. Crash landing in Boston, hours late. Time sense destroyed. I slept last in Calcutta. A strange wakefulness haunted my body. Alert to ponderous events all around me, I followed my breath as a customs official began pawing through my bag. Suddenly he stopped and handed it back to me with an apologetic smile. I felt a rising thickness in my throat to get beyond that door. She would be waiting. At first she wasn't sure she could, but after letters back and forth, she'd finally agreed.

"Wait a minute, sir." Customs wanted another look. My

Burmese shoulder bag was hidden under my shawl. They thought I was hiding something. I smiled. Dressed this way, what could I hide? They readily agreed and sent me on.

Soft mane of curly hair in my hands, warm softness and familiar sweet smell in my nostrils, bringing my head against her neck. Her eyes more dazed than mine. Who just got off the plane? She tried not to stare. Suddenly her eyes flashed like mirrors at me, and I looked for the first time. Good God! Who are you? Maybe if I talked she'd recognize me, so I filled the car with strange tales. My sister was silent in the back seat. Uncomfortably silent. Then we all were.

Another house. A room with flowers in a vase and a welcome note on the door. Some old possessions of mine transplanted here for decoration. Certainly not for familiarity. I couldn't say that I recognized any of it. Only her. The only thing that felt right, felt like it was not dissolving against my mind was her warm touch.

We sat before a fireplace full of embers. No more stories. We held each other lying on the rug. I asked her if she would stay the night. Funny, after eight years together, I had to ask. After a moment of serious struggle she acceded to the humor and accompanied me to bed.

An hour later the bridge of exquisite closeness was washed away in the flood of her misgivings, our closeness was too much for her to bear. This can't happen again, she told both of us. Her explanations were beside the point. To tell me why, really, would be excruciating for her, allowing me that access to her heart that she desperately wanted to close now to ensure our separateness. I had no elaborate objections. Something told me that this was all wrong, that we could work through it, but my reflex was to watch, as I'd been trained these last months, to be aware of pain and impermanence. Her words and her decisions were just events, further explosions. We shared tears.

"We can't be what we were to each other," she repeated over and over as we sat in the dark rooms.

"And we can't be strangers," I replied, feeling my love

bounce off a stone wall. Feeling her denial of what was there, and her refusal to gamble her denial by exploring it.

And so we even managed a final scene of good-bye.

"What happened to your testosterone?" my friend Martin asked quietly, popping the top off a cold bottle of beer. I didn't recognize the word. He offered me a glass. Beer used to be my favorite liquid but I passed. "Male hormones," he explained and the brows of his satyrlike face wrinkled. "The last time I saw you, you were in a leather jacket, five rings on your hand, a big beard, fancy scarves, and a very different look in your eye."

I looked down at my baggy sweater and overalls and black sneakers. "But it's not even the clothes, you know, or your half inch of hair or even that your beard is gone. Let me explain it this way. The priest, or whatever he's called in different locales, is readily identifiable. He wears a uniform. So his vibration, of sanctity or insanity or whatever, is readily identifiable. 'Oh, he's a priest, it's all right. A holy man.' But when people pick up on that vibration without the uniform, it's unsettling to them, even a little threatening. And you've definitely got that aspect to you."

Martin got up and walked across the kitchen to start preparing dinner. His assessment was a little difficult to comprehend, but I didn't doubt it. I had come to see him because I needed an explanation for why the surroundings I'd left not that long ago seemed so bizarre. If anyone would know, Martin would. An anthropologist, he had made three trips in the last couple of years to villages in the countryside of Nepal inhabited by refugee Tibetans, where he would spend four months at a time removed entirely from contact with Westerners, and then get on a plane and be at the Harvard Graduate School a few days later. He knew about transitions.

"It's only been six months," I began. "That's what's so hard to comprehend. I *recognize* everything, it just hasn't been that much time since all of this was my home. I lived here. But none of it is familiar any more. I'm walking in shadows. When I reach out for something, there's nothing to touch." I smiled. "Pardon the metaphors, I'm not sure I'm being very clear." Martin knew what it was like to walk in dreams. He had less belief in his surroundings than anyone I knew.

"Listen, I was walking through the Square to get here." I took a deep breath. "People are like phantoms, Martin. Can you understand that? I'm looking at a past that isn't there. Just because it's familiar doesn't give it any reality. Everything I knew is inaccessible to me. I didn't know that until the moment I landed. Really. I didn't know what I'd become." I paused, the rest of the words were really hard. "That's why splitting up with her is so much pain. She's still real for me, Martin. The only real thing I sense."

"What are you going to do now? For me it was easier just to come back and get down to work. Although it made no sense, I had fewer questions to ask. The questions have no answers, you know?" Martin poured half his bottle of beer into another glass and handed it to me.

I drank it and knew the taste, felt the memory explode as my body heated at the touch of the liquid, balanced for a moment, hesitating to judge, then swallowed it all. "I don't know. I've never been in this situation. No wife, no job, no money, no plans. Hover is back and there's a retreat starting out in western Massachusetts in about a week. I think I'll head for that."

"Here," Martin handed me a twenty dollar bill. "I'd give you more if I had it, but it's more than you've got. My contribution to the progress of the *Dharma*."

When I saw Hover about three days later, I told him everything as he sat on his pillow facing me on the floor, smiling, laughing, calm, and kinder than anyone I've ever met. He was particularly interested in my experiences in Burma and had me explain all of the phenomena in detail: my false brushes with *nirvana*, Sayama's "corrections," and my encounter with U Ba Khin. He made me explain certain terms I was using until he was sure I understood them.

All of this was kind of nice to retell. I only wished the story had ended in Rangoon. I took a deep breath and continued. I told him of my wife's decision to separate her life from mine in the only way she seemed to know how, by keeping me at such a distance that I became a stranger. As I talked I felt the water well over the edge of my eyes.

Then I told him about my plans, the academic projects I had in mind for papers on meditation.

"But," I said and heard the syllable echo hollowly in the room, "it's hard to get started on them." I stopped and shook my head, then the words just started tumbling out. "Nothing is real anymore. No, I mean everything is all of a sudden real, much too real. I stand on a street corner, gaping because everything is dissolving against my eyes. I can't look at trees anymore. They start to melt, so I turn away. I can't hear music. It's abrasive, or if I listen closely, the sound disintegrates. It just becomes a zillion tiny moments fading out of existence. And people! Hover, they're like ghosts. It's like I'm staring right through them. Their voices are like echoes. I feel like reaching out and grabbing them, but I know there's nothing to touch. And that doesn't make me peaceful or unattached, it scares the hell out of me."

"I know, I know it well. When I got back from Burma, years ago, I couldn't go near a crowd. It terrified me. I still can't but I do, if you know what I mean. After a while you start blending more, and then the confrontation becomes less acute." Then he cleared his throat and sat up straighter on his pillow and spoke like a physician who has conducted a thorough examination of the patient.

"The only thing that will end the terror is to let go. To let go of everything," he said.

The way he said the words "let go" in a half-whispering command gave me a slight shiver. It was almost like a password, an incantation, a verbal symbol for that which has no name. And the mood he evoked by that phrase was so uncharacteristic of the man whose major interest had always been effort and striving. His bald head looked to me now as though it belonged to some inscrutable Zen master. He continued, "as long as you want *nirvana*, you'll never get it. You think that once you attain that state, all your troubles are over. But it's just an event along this path. You can't live your life in the supramundane. You return to *this* state, *this* world, and it is here that the business of purification, of continuing to rid yourself of the defilements that condition future suffering takes place. *Nirvana* isn't anything special, you see? As long as you're straining, reaching, clinging, as long as you want it, you'll never get it. You just do the work, day by day, year by year, lifetime by lifetime, and it comes. And you don't have to go anywhere to find it, it's right here, right in the fear and terror."

"But even more than that," he went on, "you're clinging; you're searching for some situation, some place to stand on. Something solid under you to watch it all dissolve. You can't get started on your work until 'things settle down.'" He paused and rubbed his eyes. "I'll tell you," he said as if confiding in me, "they won't. That's not the nature of this process once it takes hold of you."

His whole demeanor began to change. He sagged a little, as if he had just put down a heavy load, the burden of teaching. "I'll tell you the truth," he began again in a matter-of-fact tone that disturbed me a little. "I don't really know what's going on here. What am I doing sitting up there? I'm no teacher of meditation. They've got the wrong man."

I stared at him incredulously. I didn't know what he had been up to since I saw him in India six months past, but if he wasn't a meditation teacher, I couldn't name one. I recalled the nervous, often uncertain person I had first met two years ago. The transformation was remarkable. From the first evening of the course in Massachusetts, I had sensed an enormous difference. The calmness in his voice. The control. The power that radiated from him like an aura.

"None of this makes sense, you see," he went on. "Meditation courses in America, taught by an engineer? Well, if I let it happen I could teach every day until next Christmas, that's how many people want it to happen. So somewhere along the line, I realized there's much more at work than I know. That my rational, reasoned decisions mean very little. In a sense this is where the path becomes much easier, and excruciatingly difficult. You realize it's not in your hands. That this thing goes on despite you. All you have to do is let go and hang on for the ride. But that becomes a subtler and subtler trick with each step you take. Well, let's go back to you now. I think you should take it easy."

I was startled. I'd never heard him give any advice except to "keep working." I wondered what I was doing wrong.

"You've been through a lot, worked your way through some big obstacles, now it's time to relax a little. Sit when you want to sit, whenever you feel like it. Help out some in the kitchen, read, have a great time. This is a beautiful place, this camp. Enjoy it. Go for walks. I'll tell you, the best atmosphere for meditation is that of a country resort."

At first I didn't know what to do with Hover's advice. It took an enormous effort to overcome the guilt and doubt of my own motivations when I skipped that afternoon's group sitting and remained in my cabin writing in my notebook. But I did it anyway, because it felt right. I started to understand that his admonition to "sit when you feel like it" meant more than the linguistic convenience implied. It forced me to focus my attention on my intuition, to make choices choicelessly, boldly, without the comforting support of authority, convention or reason. Hover was telling me to enjoy myself at a country resort and not mope along on a guided tour.

Part of enjoying myself, it seemed, was not trying to get anything done. It was important not to sit when I most wanted to, because this wanting was tied to anticipation, expectation, getting absorbed in the "next" event, the next sensation, wondering if perhaps this hour wouldn't be the one in which "it" happened. This was the time for a walk, to put aside my hungry quest for *nirvana*, which Hover had made me realize wouldn't help me anyway in dealing with my wife or finding a place to live. So when I did sit down in the hall, it was with nothing special in mind. I just sat. For an hour or sometimes more, I watched and noted as dispassionately as I could the recurrent images of eight years with a single person parade before me. The pain was stunning, like a dentist's drill on an unanesthetized tooth. All the anxiety, shadow fears, fantasy, and nameless terrors I had met during the past six months seemed like preliminary bouts to this main event. Its tangibility, the hardness of the fact of my wife's departure from my life seemed overwhelming to face. I would close my eyes and as soon as I relaxed my mind the thoughts would crush me like an avalanche. I couldn't move from under them, couldn't place my attention elsewhere. I wished for some knot in my neck to divert me from the fire of my mind, and I smiled bitterly as I recalled the moments of bliss in Ceylon when it seemed so clear that the pain was over.

It was confusing to search for a place to live because whenever I thought about it there was no apparent reason in the world why I left Burma and Ceylon at all. *The unfinished business of my marriage with P*, I recalled my own decision. Now that had been so quickly concluded and I found myself in the cold, inhospitable dampness of early spring in New England. It was hard to put my energy into settling down here. I would rather be back in the forest. I tried to lay that thought aside, but it was much easier to figure out ways to raise money for an airline ticket than to find a home.

The easiest and most painless solution was just to stay where I was staying, at the farm with the people who had first brought me to meditation. Over the past years we had become friends, and after Cambridge the farm was the only place I could consider going upon my return to America. A couple of the residents had taken Hover's course with me, and afterward I returned to the farm with them. Following a number of days occupied by long empty walks in the woods, I had asked if I might live at the farm.

They politely declined. So I was a visitor until I could find a place of my own. I focused a little frantically on that goal. Finally I got some help from a person who proved to be my unlikeliest teacher of all.

His name was Arnie, and though he was twenty-four years old, he could have been mistaken for a high school student, with his smooth cheeks, short, parted hair and face of sweet innocence. To look at him was to see very little going on, so little that the first impulse was to confuse his appearance with his essence.

Two years ago he had done several meditation courses with Goenka. Since returning from India, he had worked as an attendant at a state mental hospital, living in a small house on the grounds and spending an average of eight or nine hours a day sitting alone, not in contact with anyone else involved in the practice. Slowly, often painfully, as he recounted to me one day, much of what drives us round and round the wheel of suffering was burnt out of his being. He watched desire arise and pass, arise and pass, over and over again until its insubstantiality was apparent, and its hold was lost. With a sense of childlike wonder, he described the experience of sitting one day and feeling on an absolute level of experience that he was *not* there. That his entire being was a process which he was neither in control of nor being controlled by. He looked at me and shook his head. "What a burden to put down. Really."

Then one day, Arnie told me, he decided that it was time to share some of what he had accumulated with others. He decided he wanted to help organize a course and he found out about my friends at the farm. When he learned of my recent events, his large, brown, faintly luminous eyes were full of such sympathetic understanding that I breathed my first sign of relief since returning to America. Now he was here to help me find a home.

"Ready?" he asked as he got out of his car. "I've got a few places to show you and some people you should meet."

I nodded with trepidation. I would rather have spent the day meditating in my room, but he lured me out with the hope that

I might find a place to live. That seemed crucial to me. I got in the car and when I slammed the door shut I felt safe for the first time in days. "Too many people," I muttered.

Our first stop was a Quaker meeting house where I sat through silence, speeches, and songs, which all sounded the same to me. People. Why were people frightening to me now? I kept hearing things. Noises coming from minds. And I couldn't tell if it was their mind or mine shouting rudely. I longed for that forest hut, or the cell in Rangoon, where the noise was so readily transparent.

My mind's dialague was interrupted by Arnie tugging at my elbow. The room was dispersing. Arnie led me out to the lawn where a group had assembled to listen to some kids playing guitars and singing. I felt more comfortable with my eyes closed, but when I heard her voice they opened. Strange, I thought, that she should look so much like my wife. Broad shoulders and curly hair, how long does it take to forget? And then in the most rapid sequence, my mind digested her completely and spun out long fantasies of introductions, conversations, and seduction. When the music stopped, I nudged Arnie, "Do you know her?" I whispered.

He nodded and smiled sympathetically. "She lives with that guy over there."

I felt a deep sinking within my body, as if my throat were working its way down into my chest. Why did that little news hurt so much? The pain that came from looking at this woman was not caused by her being unobtainable, but by the mind-body sensation of wanting her, the experience of cells stretching and grasping, mind fiber rubbing against itself deliciously. This was pure pain.

"Arnie, have you been together with a woman lately?" We sat on a bench in the empty hallway. The congregation had gone its many ways.

"I used to have very intense relationships with women," he said. "In fact one lasted through my trip to India. That's one of the reasons I came back here. But I think it's finished now, that need. It wasn't easy. It would be hard for me to describe the pain of sitting and watching that need for days and months. Feeling tears dripping down my face and not knowing what they were for. But then it passed, and I don't feel that anymore."

It was a key moment for me. I had to look at Arnie and I had to look at myself, and how we looked alike. How much alike, and how much that frightened me. Did I want to lead the kind of monastic life in America that Arnie did? I remembered my friend Martin's comment about my loss of testosterone. "She reminds you of your wife," Arnie said with a soft smile of sympathy. "Watch out for ladies with guitars. Watch out for your memory. Nothing in itself can remind you of anything. Only you can. You can choose. It's surprising how much choice we have in suffering. Just watch it a little and you'll see."

Could I choose to be Arnie? Would my face ever be that radiant? My mind that simple and loving? I wanted to ask what it feels like not to want. But the question was superfluous. All I had to do was watch Arnie and others around him. People who'd never heard of meditation gravitated to him. My lady rock singer, fantasy herself, standing beside him, unself-consciously linking her arm in his, sweet ease on her face, void of tension, and yet something powerful passing between them. Love. Arnie's quiet love.

We weren't in a huge rush to move on. Arnie sat quite still. "I still feel drained after being in crowds of people for a while." I nodded vigorously. That faint sense of street corner exhaustion, like a late summer thundercloud in the air. Oppressive: hot, confining; a sensation that made you feel a need to escape.

But Arnie's remarks contained none of that. This was where our shared understanding ended. Where my own understanding strained to comprehend him. He was drained, he was fatigued. But *behind* that, he was just the way he always was. And me? Inside the fatigue produced a huge urge to flee.

I stood up. Arnie followed. We had a list of people to see that afternoon, all possibilities for me to find that place to live alone, which seemed absolutely essential. By late afternoon, though, none of them led to anything and I was exhausted. We started driving back to the farm.

"Far out," Arnie said as he made an unexpected turn off the road. "I forgot this place was here." He pulled the car over to the side of the road and I followed him into a variety store. It was getting on in the afternoon and we still had several stops to make. "What do you want in here?" I asked.

He shrugged, "Let's see what they've got."

It was hard to say. Boxes of merchandise were piled everywhere, in absolutely no order, floor to ceiling. Empty cartons filled the corners. A T.V. set was perched above the counter, chattering the football game like a caged parrot. The owner a round, balding pop-eyed, old-time New Englander, recognized Arnie and reported at great length the news of this area and in particular an automobile accident involving someone Arnie knew.

Arnie seemed to melt into the chaos. He chomped contentedly on a chocolate Ring Ding and some potato chips. I was afraid I'd never pry him loose. Another customer finally came in and took the owner off in search of laundry soap.

"Nice place," Arnie said when we were outside. "Nice it would be to work there." Then he said quite cheerily, "Have you had enough of banging your head against the wall?" I looked at him incredulously. "You look like a little mouse lost in a big field running around trying to find a hole. You're never going to find anything until you learn how to sit still."

His smile was perfectly serious. A serious smile. It forced me to gather my attention. I realized that for the first time all day I was becoming aware of my state of mind, its totally indulgent preoccupation with the goal of *getting a place to live*. I almost laughed. Arnie had been humoring me all day.

"You weren't trying to find a place at all, were you?" I said.

He shrugged. "If we had found one, we would have found one. I didn't think the chances were particularly good considering the shape of your mind, but you had to find that out."

"Well, what do you think I should do?" I asked.

"Do? I don't think you should do anything. Or rather, I think you should try to understand that you *can't* do anything. When you know that, it'll do itself. See, you missed a lot of good opportunities today. I introduced you to some very good people, and there were moments when you could have learned a lot, but you were set on finding a place to live. That's what today was programmed for. So you missed a lot."

We were stopped at a red light. He pointed again. "The light turns and we go, but can you understand, there's nothing out there. Nothing. We move from nothing to nothing. As if we were stepping out of a spaceship into absolute, empty darkness. No up or down and the boundaries are infinite. That's reality. Not the spaceship. That's a toy. You want to find yourself some spaceship to navigate in. Forget it. All you'll get is glimpses through the portholes."

Arnie's voice had a quiet earnestness, a kind of joyful understanding that I'd never heard from anyone before. "Don't you see, all situations are empty, they have no weight, no significance. So if you watch, then everything has something to teach you. Nothing is wasted. Everything is useful. I don't know why you're back here in America and not in India. But as long as you keep asking yourself that, you're wasting the chance to find out."

Epilogue:

Manjushri's Burden

I SET THE CHAIN saw down on the stump of the tree which I had just felled and sat down on the log to drink from my canteen. It was the very same orange water bag I had purchased to take with me to India two years ago. I looked up through the bare November trees at the sun edging toward the apex of its low autumn arc. Then I looked at the piles of cordwood I'd accumulated along the road during the past months. There would certainly be enough for the stoves before the first snowfall. Satisfied, I picked up my saw and headed back to the house.

This was a very quiet time on the farm with not many people around. Others who had been here before me had moved on, and recently I'd become chief caretaker and homesteader. When I had first come here as a visitor while looking around the county for a home, I was politely tolerated by the small group of residents on the farm but considered too strange to stay. The strangeness faded, however, and I found my home. Now, here

I was taking care of a cow, cutting wood, fixing stone walls, and building cabinets.

After a few more chores, I finally set out on the long drive up the coast of Maine to the small town where an American teacher of *vipassana* named Joseph Goldstein was leading an intensive three-month retreat in a former Catholic seminary. It was late afternoon, and I was a little behind schedule. There was always a lot to do now. Living had become an endless series of chores, with sitting twice a day just another item on the list. I felt a little guilty about taking this weekend off when there was still so much to do at the farm before winter rolled in. But this was important, too.

Joseph Goldstein had studied and practiced in India for years and then, without fanfare, he had begun giving retreats in America. Without jargon, Joseph translates Buddha's *Dharma* into a penetratingly direct examination of who we are, and his ability to communicate the practice of *vipassana* simply, directly, and with a great power has led to a constant flow of new students, those with no connection to India, exotic locales, religion, or even Buddhism. I had spent a lot of time with him the past winter in California, and he had become both friend and teacher. I'd learned from him in both respects. He had taught me that it is unnecessary to go to a particular place, a dark room or to India, to find truth. *What is,* that is *Dharma.* And so I'd begun to work with what is, with my friends and my surroundings. I'd learned that desire isn't something to squash or run from, but something to untangle carefully, mindfully, and never without pain. So friendship and work and intimacy with women had returned to my life. The Quest for enlightenment remained, but it was no longer what I had envisioned in Ceylon. It was now just little steps to untangle the mind.

When I arrived at the place of the retreat in Bucksport, near Bar Harbor, it was already late into a starry night. After collecting my gear and locking the car, I prepared to head for the main building, but I was stopped by the sound of slow footfalls against a background of stillness. Figures dressed in baggy, white yogi pants and ski parkas were walking silently, with heads bowed, in the open courtyard. They were engaged in the specific meditation practice of mindfulness of walking, awareness of each step. They moved in slow motion. I became self-consciously aware of the tempo of my life and the state of my mind. All the way up here my mind had been filled with plans for Monday morning back on the farm, building this, fixing that. But here there was stillness, an atmosphere I remembered from Ceylon and Burma. I leaned back against my car, and as I watched the walking figures one of them approached. Almost shyly, he stood before me, looked into my eyes and then, with one brief smile, departed. When he had gone I realized that I had known him briefly in California.

My friend's gaze set me back. It was the empty look of one absorbed in each detail of the present moment. He rises, dresses, washes, sits and walks, I thought. Someone else puts food before him, cleans his clothes, and turns up the heat. His mind poised in the moment cuts through the shadows of fear and desire that arise in the darkness of the meditation hall. For him, I mused, existence is simple and beautiful; knowledge is exquisite.

I was conscious of my cynicism. I had deliberately left my flowing yogi pants at home, where they had been packed away for some time now. The blue jeans I was wearing were loose enough to sit in and more practical for other things. I had discovered that when you step out of the darkness, the shadows disappear and the form is there. The street corner is real. You can scream until you're blue in the face that it's a cosmic illusion, but the sinking, thrashing, grasping sensation in the gut bloating up as you watch a woman walk by whose physical body calls you *is real*. She is real. I am real. My desire is real. And so is my discomfort with that desire.

For months after my return I had lived in fear. Fear of what my senses would come in contact with. Fear of my reactions. Fear that I had lost the protection of the walls, of walls like these, in this place, that had enabled me to watch my mind only a bit at a time.

I watched my friend slowly walking in the shadows. Another month and the lease on this place would be up. Then his pain would begin.

One day Joseph and I walked up the road that leads away from the seminary. The sky was purple with quick moving clouds, and the presence of the sea could be sensed in the air and in the dwarf vegetation.

"You get hooked so easily on the quietness of your mind in the monastic environment," I said, voicing the consternation with this place that had been growing since I arrived. "You avoid your *karma*, but you're not free from it."

Joseph smiled. "But without deep experience in the quietness, you'll never even know what karma is. We live in a world of concepts, a world of shadows. So we come into an environment like this to see beyond the concepts. You have no choices to make here. No relationships to make. No noise and very few words. So sooner or later *how* the mind works must start to make itself clear. You start to see through the ephemeral nature of your mind's concepts *about* how things are. You start to see *how* things are. You begin to approach the creator of the concepts."

"But then what happens when you go outside the walls, back into the world of concepts?" I wasn't challenging him. I wanted to know. The stillness that Joseph radiated no matter where I saw him, in a crowd or in a silent room, said that he might tell me.

"Watch out for the easy distinction between the *world* out there and what is in here," he said. "Wisdom is just the ability to listen. Listen to your mind. Completely. This is an artificial environment for sure. There's nothing particularly *significant*, or good, or holy, or even Buddhist about walls and silence and no food after noon. Just a set of circumstances that help the process of listening.

"So you think this is a better place to gain wisdom, in this kind of environment?" I asked.

Joseph shook his head. "Wisdom is a quality of mind. It

doesn't matter what you are looking at. In here there is always the danger that people get caught by quietness. Out there, you get caught in different ways, by events, people, emotions. They distract you in the real sense. You forget their phenomenal, impermanent nature. The mind solidifies. You stop listening. So sometimes you're out there and sometimes in here, and always the task is the same."

The long walk felt good. I had spent the day before just sitting around in stuffy rooms chatting with the teachers and good friends. I realized how my body of late had become like a workhorse that loses its timing without daily exercise. I had come to take a certain pride in the lean muscles that had developed recently working each day with my body. I'd begun to feel very at home, relaxed in my body. For months after my return from India I had felt like a strange corpse. As if I was a prisoner in someone else's body.

"So how are things on the farm?" The question came from a friend named Richard who was the manager of this whole show. He'd spent a good part of the summer with us at the farm getting the retreat organized. For some two months now, he had been up here, where he was responsible for the material existence of some seventy meditators. He lit a cigarette and leaned back in his chair, peering at me through gold wire rimmed glasses. "So what have you been up to? It's taken you a while to get up here."

"A lot to do these days, you know," I shrugged. "Yesterday the cow decided to topple the gate to her pasture."

"You should stay up here a little longer." he said. I felt his eyes checking me for something. "This show takes a little time to appreciate. It's quite a powerful event."

"I find it a little disconcerting, really. I'm just being honest with you, Richard. I'm more deeply committed to my meditation practice now than I've ever been. But it means more to me right now than just sitting. It means putting myself in situations, hard situations where the garbage of my mind becomes apparent to me. Not masking it in silence. Listening to it scream. For me this is the next step, the logical one. When the cow smashes the fence, or the people I live with leave their dirty dishes all over or wake up on the wrong side of bed, there's no Noble Silence to protect me. Or when I start to get close to a woman and feel her fear and mine. I want to see my fear. I want to face it. Don Juan's warrior is the image I put on my altar these days."

Richard nodded. "I hear you. I really do. I could see that coming last summer. But since you've gotten back from sitting again with Hover you've really polished up your act. Impeccable. That's part of the way of the warrior Don Juan tries to teach Castaneda. I notice it in the way you dress these days, the way you build fences. But you know, there's another part to the teaching of the warrior. Impeccability can't stand alone. A big game hunter can be impeccable. A wise man has to be more. A warrior has to know something. Real impeccability comes from controlled folly. Emptiness. No self. You have to know that all actions are meaningless gestures. That there's nothing there to gain or achieve. But you do it anyway. Impeccably. Not even for the sake of impeccability. For absolutely nothing." Richard paused and stubbed out his cigarette. He rarely finished one. "What is it you want out there?"

My body stiffened. "Nothing," I answered, listening hard to my own words for the answer, "except the end of fear."

A deep brass gong sounded, the sound of Benares, Ceylon, Burma. The call for group meditation. Richard didn't move. "Desire is very subtle, and endless," he finally replied.

I hadn't yet been in the meditation hall. As I entered now I knew I'd been avoiding it. The high ceiling spaciousness seemed to swallow me. Even as I closed my eyes sitting on my pillow my mind was no longer racing, my entire being was. Against the backdrop of powerful silence, certain facts, details, qualities of nature were more readily discernible. Like the evanescence of my being.

I'd been running from that fact for a while, in dark caves and jungles chasing some elusive Ultimate Truth, some state of being that would set me free. Now I was scared out of my pants to find it right over my shoulder. Pursuing me. Would I get away again? My body wouldn't move. I had the sense that nothing is solid, nothing can be touched or held, that reality is so different from my fantasy of bliss. It's not bliss, it's terrifying, because reality has no room for *me*. To know reality *I* must die. And as I sat on my cushion I felt the rising speed of chaos, impermanence, dissolution, not as something to be watched as I had all these months, but as something to participate in. Reality is not a spectator sport.

Late Sunday afternoon, Richard walked me to the car. "You think you'll make it back up here before its all over?" he asked.

I shook my head. "You know I don't believe in this here meditation stuff."

He nodded, "Oh, right, I forgot." Just before I got in the car he stopped me. "One more story. For the road." He smiled, as if asking if I was ready. "In Tibetan Buddhism the *Boddhisattva* of Wisdom is named Manjushri. He's the one who helps beings through the door of enlightenment. So here's the story. A monk has been practicing at a monastery for many years. No go. He's not getting anywhere, he thinks. He's still not free. He's frustrated. He resolves to gain enlightenment or die trying. There's a high mountain, and he decided to scale it in search of enlightenment. As the monk is climbing the mountain he sees a really old man dressed in rags, descending the mountain bent under the weight of a huge sack on his back. It is Manjushri but the Monk doesn't know it, all he sees is an old man with a burden. He's about to pass right by when he catches the old man's eyes. He's not sure but he thinks he sees something there. He asks the old man what he knows about enlightenment. The old man just looks at him without a word. His hands loosen and he lets the bag drop from his shoulders. The moment the sack hits the ground the monks sees. He sees it all. The absoluteness of that moment, nothing else. No mountain to climb, no journey to make. The moment the bag is dropped the monk is free. It is his enlightenment. So now what does he do? There's no mountain to climb. He just looks at Manjushri without a word. "Now what?" He wants to know. Quite calmly the old man picks up the sack, bends again under the heavy load and struggles on down the mountain."

Richard paused and lit a cigarette. "A very good story," he commented. "Most people doing this meditation practice like to hear it. I'm not sure they hear all of it. See, on the first level the story has a deep truth. Okay, enlightenment isn't on some mountain top. Its right where you're standing with the bag on your shoulders. And the moment after is just the next moment. You pick up the sack again and proceed. Very good. Nothing to gain, nowhere to go. Chop wood and haul water as they say in Zen. Give up your useless striving. But there's a little bit more to the story, at least as I hear it. The enlightenment itself. The dropping of the bag. What it means to let go of that burden. Many of us have had the experience of loosening our grip, feeling the bag start to slip out of our hands, that moment when there is nothing to grab onto. Not a pleasant feeling. But a powerful one. And then its all back to normal. The terror is past, we've picked up the bag again. We're ready to resume, with wisdom this time." Richard stepped on his half finished cigarette. "But did we drop the bag? Did we really let it go? Did we hear the thud and then wait for the echos to die, completely until there was nothing? Or did we just imagine it?"

I looked up and it was sunset. I'd be driving back in near total darkness. It would be a long ride.

Baylor 8/9/77